making work
at home work

making work at home work

successfully growing a business and a family under one roof

mary m. byers

Revell

a division of Baker Publishing Group
Grand Rapids, Michigan

Published by Revell
a division of Baker Publishing Group
P.O. Box 6287, Grand Rapids, MI 49516-6287
www.revellbooks.com

Printed in the United States of America

Library of Congress Cataloging-in-Publication Data
Byers, Mary M., 1962–
    Making work at home work : successfully growing a business and a family
under one roof / Mary M. Byers.
        p.   cm.
    Includes bibliographical references.
    ISBN 978-0-8007-3275-2 (pbk.)
    1. Home-based businesses. 2. Working mothers. I. Title.
HD62.38.B94 2009
658′.0412—dc22   2008049312

Unless otherwise indicated, Scripture is taken from the HOLY BIBLE, NEW INTER-NATIONAL VERSION®. NIV®. Copyright © 1973, 1978, 1984 by International Bible Society. Used by permission of Zondervan. All rights reserved.

Scripture marked KJV is taken from the King James Version of the Bible.

Recipes on pages 204–10 are from *The Great American Supper Swap* by Trish Berg and are used by permission of David C. Cook, Colorado Springs, CO. All rights reserved. For copies of this book call 800-323-7543 (or online at www.davidccook.com).

Recipes on pages 210–18 are from *Once-a-Month Cooking: Revised and Expanded* by Mimi Wilson and Mary Beth Lagerborg. Copyright © 2007 by the authors and reprinted by permission of St. Martin's Press, LLC.

Published in association with the literary agency of Alive Communications, Inc., 7680 Goddard Street, Suite 200, Colorado Springs, CO 80920. www.alivecommunications.com

To Marissa and Mason—
you are why I work at home.
And to Stuart—
you make it possible.

I love you all deeply.
Thanks for being a part of both my home and business team!

contents

work-at-home mom profiles

acknowledgments

I am grateful to be able to do work I love and to do it from home. It's not easy, but my path has been sprinkled with wonderful family and friends who encourage, love, and support me. I am blessed. Please do not be offended if you do not see your name on this page. I am who I am because of who I know. And I've been touched by many people over the years, all of whom have helped create the person I am today. The following have been especially helpful as I worked on this project.

Beth Jusino, my literary agent, and Jennifer Leep, my editor, helped craft this idea. I'm grateful to be in partnership with you.

Sarah Albracht, Tracy Dowell, and Pat Essig were all generous in sharing their experience in the field of network marketing. Thanks for enlightening me!

I'm indebted to adviser June Walker for sharing her tax wisdom with those of us who work from home.

Because I am not an accountant or financial planner, I asked several individuals to review the chapter on retirement planning to be sure I don't lead you astray. Thanks to the following who helped in this regard: Cindy Sumner, speaker and author of *Dol-*

lars and Sense: A Mom's Guide to Money Matters; John Sumner, president, Sumner National Bank; Michelle J. Usher, CPA and manager, Sikich LLP; Andrew Paoni, MBA, vice president, Sikich Cozad Asset Management, LLC; and Brent Davis, AAMS, Edward Jones Investments.

Special thanks to the 125 women who responded to an online survey about the challenges of working from home, and to the two dozen more who candidly shared their experiences with me in person.

Special thanks to Bob Rechner, executive director at the Illinois State Dental Society and my former boss, who continues to be an extraordinary mentor and friend and who provided me with my first work-at-home contract. (Are we really old enough to have known each other for twenty years?) I'm also indebted to Bill Zepp, CAE, executive director of the Oregon Dental Association, for being one of the first individuals to hire me after I "retired." You helped launch my business.

As always, Julie Kaiser and Tara McAndrew, my beloved fellow writers, checked in occasionally to make sure I was still alive. Julie and my mom, Nancy Carlson, also proofed the manuscript for me. Thanks for loaning me your eyes and expertise as I neared the end of the project. Julie also helped with the work-at-home mom profiles you'll see throughout this book. (And Mom, thanks for the soup that kept showing up for lunch at just the right times! More importantly, thanks for being so generous with your encouragement over the years.)

Finally, to work-at-home moms everywhere: the path is hard, the pay may not be great, and the tangible benefits may be sorely lacking, but the intangible benefits are rewarding beyond measure. Be strong. Stay the course. And don't forget that time invested in your family is never wasted.

introduction

One of the hardest decisions I ever made was to leave full-time employment outside the home in order to be more available to my children.

One of the hardest things I've ever done is to run a home-based business—also to be more available to my children.

If you too have experienced the challenges of successfully growing a business and a family under one roof, this book is for you.

The genesis of this book was rather simple. It began as my quest to more fully understand the dynamics of balancing work and family when they coexist under one roof.

I understand that balance is an issue most of today's working mothers wrestle with. However, a large portion of working women leave home to make their living. What about those of us who have a short commute down the hallway? There's a big difference between heading to an office each day—with the child care support system this necessitates—and doing your work with children underfoot or hovering in the background.

In my own search for practical guidance about working from home, I discovered that though it's easy to find resources to help women decide what type of home-based business to start, it's not as easy to find resources about sustaining both a home and a business *after* the start-up phase. This lack of information was what led me to write *Making Work at Home Work*.

If you're like me, you've discovered that starting your business was the easy part. It's keeping your business going while meeting your family commitments that's difficult. Though I've been in business for myself for over a decade, there are still days when I wonder, *Why am I doing this?* It's hard to be a wife, mother, and CEO—and to be equally good at all of these jobs, especially during a busy season of work. There have been many times when I thought it would be easier to let the business slide so that I could focus more fully on my family or conversely to check out temporarily on my family when the demands of business required more attention. But I believe that my home-based business is a perfect provision for me and my family. It allows me to do work I love, contribute to the family income, use the skills I have, and most importantly, have flexibility in my schedule, which is precious to me.

I've relied on a cadre of other working mothers to provide input and feedback to help ensure that this book is helpful and practical and one you'll turn to time and time again. (That's my hope, anyway!) Over 125 work-at-home mothers responded to an online survey with questions designed to explore the heart of work-at-home issues. More than two dozen women also shared in person the joys and struggles they encounter as they work from home.

Though our reasons for working may be different, I believe the challenges we encounter are similar. I also passionately believe we can learn from one another, which is why I took the time to listen to other work-at-home moms. I learned from them and look forward to sharing this knowledge with you.

Regardless of why you're working, the challenge of doing so with children underfoot tests even the smartest, bravest, most organized, most multitasking mamas around. I have yet to hear a work-at-home mom describe the job as "easy." That's because meeting your family's needs while meeting your business requirements can be mutually exclusive. Locking yourself in your office to make an important deadline requires disconnecting from your family. Packing your wares to head to a friend's house for a direct sales party may mean not getting to read to your kids at bedtime or kiss them good night. And preparing your financial reports each month requires concentration that's not possible with a toddler in your lap. (Okay, okay, I don't always keep up with my financial data every month either, even though I know I should.)

The point is that as at-home entrepreneurs, we've chosen a path that is more difficult to traverse than it might be if we had an office outside the home. I know that outside employment has challenges of its own, but that's not what this book is about. It *is* about the joy and pain of being able to work in your pajamas; the conflict that occurs when you love both your work and your family but the title of CEO belongs to you; the challenge of working enough to make a profit without becoming consumed; and the heartbreak of hearing a child say, "I hate your job!" as one woman confided her son had done. It's about navigating the white waters of marriage when one or both partners are self-employed, figuring out how to get your kids where they need to be at the same time you need to deliver a sales order, and the guilt all moms feel when they believe they've let their kids down.

If you want to explore what it really means to run a home-based business while raising a family, then you're right where you need to be. I invite you to pour yourself a favorite beverage, grab a highlighter, curl up in your preferred reading spot, and be ready to be transformed both as a mother and as a home-based business owner.

We'll examine two aspects of having a home-based business: preserving your profit and saving your sanity—under one roof. I believe that if you're able to do each of these things, then you'll have both a successful family and a successful home-based business to show for it.

Though success shouldn't be defined only by dollars and cents, if you're going to be working in a home-based business, which requires time away from your family, you might as well make a profit as well as benefiting from the other reasons you work.

This book will show you how it's possible to have both profit and your sanity—at the same time! We'll focus on saving your sanity in the first half of the book and on making a profit in the second half. If you're more concerned about profit right now, however, feel free to turn to the second half and begin reading there. Then you can come back to the beginning and join us here.

In addition to sharing my own experience, I'm pleased to be able to share profiles of a dozen other work-at-home moms. I loved learning about their businesses as well as benefiting from their advice. Their stories are sprinkled throughout the book. I hope you'll enjoy these snapshots of fellow at-home entrepreneurs.

More than anything, I want this book to meet you where you are and to be helpful to you, regardless of whether you've been in business for a decade or a month. Home business success *is* possible, and I want you to experience it in all its fullness.

saving
your
sanity

1

being honest

acknowledging the difference between "at home" and "work at home"

I left full-time employment outside the home to be more available to my children. I remember calling my friend Dana to tell her I had resigned from my job to become an at-home mom.

There was silence on the other end of the line.

After a long pause, Dana asked, "You'll freelance, won't you?"

Frankly, the decision to leave work had left me so emotionally exhausted, I hadn't even gotten around to thinking about what I would "do" once I got home. Clearly, Dana was shocked. Being an at-home mom had never occurred to her at that point, even though she had bravely navigated the challenge of birthing twins. (That's enough to make me want to lie down and take a yearlong nap!)

I answered Dana's question by mumbling something profound like, "Yeah, I probably will," even though I had no such intention. I had to save face somehow. (I take great joy in the fact that Dana is now also a work-at-home mom. She took the skills she used previously in the marketplace to launch a meeting planning business that's thriving. More importantly, she gets to spend time with her two beautiful daughters, Erin and Julie.)

Dana is not alone in her inability to imagine heading home. I didn't even think of it as a possibility until my friend Libby stepped off the fast track to focus on her two kids, Alex and Claire. I'm embarrassed to admit that once, when we met for lunch (me in my professional business attire and she in her decidedly more comfy "mom" clothes), I actually had the audacity to ask her, "So how do you spend your days?" because I was insanely curious about what "at-home" moms did all day.

It wasn't until I saw Libby—an educated, talented woman whom I knew personally—decide to trade a briefcase for a diaper bag that I even began to think about it. (Eventually Libby also became an at-home entrepreneur, making exquisite beaded and hand-crafted sterling silver jewelry and working for an accounting firm on a contractual basis.)

This leads to my story.

I left employment outside the home several months prior to my second child's birth. My former employer was kind enough to ask me to do some freelance work. That was the beginning of my work-at-home career. My son was in utero, my daughter was close to two at the time and still taking naps, and I found I enjoyed the stimulation of working for a couple of hours each day while she slept.

After the birth of my son, a colleague who needed a speaker for a meeting called. I live in central Illinois. The meeting was in the state of Virginia. At a resort. I'd be gone for two nights. Alone. In a hotel room. No crying babies and no midnight feeding. It sounded pretty good. Mustering every ounce of professionalism I possessed, I told him I'd "check my schedule and get back with him"—even though I knew before hanging up what my answer would be.

The only things on my schedule were changing diapers and cooking meals. In fact, that's all I had on the calendar for the next six months.

I talked to my husband, who gave me his blessing to accept the engagement. He bravely offered to hold down the fort while I was gone. At the time, neither of us realized we were starting a business. And that's how I became an at-home entrepreneur.

> Though all moms work at home, there's a key difference between an at-home mom and one who works at home for a profit: one has responsibilities to clients and customers in addition to family.

Your journey as a work-at-home mom may be similar—or you may have been more intentional about starting a home-based business. In either case, there's a work-at-home success principle that's more important than anything else you need to know. *Though all moms work at home, there's a key difference between an at-home mom and one who works at home for a profit: one has responsibilities to clients and customers in addition to family.* Recognizing this difference is essential both to your sanity and to your family's well-being.

Early in my at-home career, though I was a work-at-home mom, *I still thought of myself as an at-home mom.* In retrospect, I can see that I made an error that many work-at-home moms make: I wasn't honest with myself. I was running a business while telling myself—and those around me—that I was an at-home mom. I was working without the support system that moms who work outside the home have. I didn't have child care. I simply expected that I'd be able to continue to do everything—even as the business kept growing.

As business piled up I continued to try to juggle my family needs with my business needs. I woke up before my kids to put in writing time. I worked during nap time. I stayed up late at night to finish projects and meet assigned deadlines. Then I'd wake up and do it all over again. It took a toll on me physically. It took a toll on my marriage. Being the stubborn "can-do" woman that I am, however,

I soldiered on. When I couldn't get everything done or give every-thing the attention it needed, I berated myself for not being more organized and more productive and challenged myself to work harder. I couldn't understand why I wasn't able to "do it all." I was a work-at-home mom with an at-home attitude.

You know the saying: if mama ain't happy, ain't nobody happy.

I was home with my kids, where I wanted to be, but I was mis-erable. I was torn between my business life and my home life, but I couldn't get away from either since both were under the same roof. Working at home wasn't working.

After living through a holiday season that held no joy and only the stress of marking things off my to-do list, I realized that my failure to acknowledge myself as a "work-at-home" mom was doing damage to me and my family. It made me think I was readily avail-able to volunteer for anything and everything, launder a needed jersey on short notice, sew on Girl Scout patches within one hour of receiving them, run errands anytime, and participate in every one of my kids' field trips. All that *and* write two monthly columns, edit and proofread a forty-page association magazine, coordinate the production of two newsletters, research and develop new speaking presentations, and write a book.

Oh, yeah. Did I mention having dinner on the table every night?

The reality is that very few, if any, mothers (at-home or not) have the kind of availability I expected of myself. I was a victim of my own faulty thinking. When I realized the danger in doing this, I made the decision to start thinking of myself as a work-at-home mom.

That was the beginning of saving my sanity.

The shift was subtle, but as a work-at-home mom, I now under-stand that I need to consider work deadlines before I say yes to any-thing. I know that sometimes work has to come before other things I'd like to do. And I also know I have to work a minimum number of hours each week to keep from falling behind in my business.

Now that my schedule reflects these three realities, being a work-at-home mom isn't nearly as frustrating or overwhelming as it used to be. Today I'm mastering my business instead of letting it master me.

Being honest regarding your work-at-home status is key to your success as well.

Do you think of yourself as an at-home mom or a work-at-home mom? The difference may seem small, but it's not. When you work at home, you have commitments to clients or customers outside the home. This adds to your to-do list and complicates your days. When you recognize and acknowledge this additional dimension of your life, however, you begin to plan your days differently, which is why being honest with yourself, your family, and your friends is essential to the success of your business.

Perception is indeed reality. When you perceive yourself as an at-home CEO, you'll be more likely to act (and plan) like one. Doing so is the difference between an out-of-control business and a controlled one.

Are you minimizing your business and the resulting income *simply because it is secondary to your primary role as mother*? Whether you make six dollars or six figures as a work-at-home mom, that income is the result of your precious time, talent, and hard work. You deserve credit for producing it. But how many times have you caught yourself saying or thinking things like the following?

- I don't make much money.
- I don't really care about making money; I just enjoy the work.
- The money is just icing on the cake for me.
- Our "extras" come from this income. (As if the extras aren't important too.)
- I'll work around the family's schedules. (What about when the schedule changes?)

When we minimize our roles as work-at-home mothers or how we came to be at-home entrepreneurs, we also minimize our skills, talents, and abilities. In addition, we diminish the positive aspects of working at home, whether it is the mental stimulation we crave, the personal growth we experience as a business owner, or the ability to contribute to our family monetarily as well as emotionally and physically.

It was liberating for me to finally be able to say, "I work at home." When those words began coming out of my mouth, I began to do things differently and working at home began working.

This may seem like a minor issue, but I purposely introduced this concept first because *when you think of yourself as an at-home CEO, you're more likely to manage your business like one. You'll control it rather than letting it control you.*

> When you think of yourself as an at-home CEO, you're more likely to manage your business like one.

You don't have to choose between having a great business and having a great family. To grow both successfully, however, you must be honest about the task you've undertaken. Managing work and family under one roof isn't easy. But in the end, the rewards are worth it. Deciding to be home with my children was a step I took in order to live without regret. My family remains my number one priority. That won't change.

What has changed in my career as a work-at-home mom is how I think about myself and what I'm doing. Minimizing my business certainly wasn't the answer. In fact, it made everything much more difficult. Being honest about what I am doing—and why I am doing it—was the first step to creating harmony between work and family. Being honest enabled me to find the balance that was so sorely lacking in my early years as an at-home entrepreneur.

Are you minimizing your work or trying to make it invisible so as not to "bother" your family? If so, are you ready to be honest about it? Doing so is an essential step in preserving your profit and saving your sanity. Acknowledging that you're a work-at-home mom rather than hiding the fact will:

- make it possible to find balance because you'll begin to consider everything on your to-do list rather than trying to squeeze the business in solely around family activities and needs;
- encourage you to recruit or hire the help you need to get your work done, whether it's arranging for child care, household help, or subcontracting services to support your business;
- provide the opportunity to involve your family in the business and to teach your children a skill set they might not otherwise learn;
- allow you to set necessary limitations on your time and how you divide it outside of work and family;
- enable friends and family to better understand the demands on your schedule and the pressures you're under and permit you to more easily ask for their help when you need it;
- elevate your business so that it receives the time and attention it needs—not at the expense of your family but in addition to it.

If you're an at-home entrepreneur with an at-home mom attitude, now's the time for an adjustment. It's essential that from now on you use the words "work-at-home" when describing yourself or thinking about your business. Doing so is the first step to finding the balance you need and want as a work-at-home entrepreneur.

And remember, if mama's happy, then everyone else is more likely to be happy too.

Lesson Learned: Honesty is the best policy. If you work from home for profit, acknowledge it. Trying to make your work invisible to your family or others likely will make you miserable and make preserving your profit and saving your sanity more difficult than it has to be.

My Work-at-Home Mom Profile

Name and type of business:

Mary Byers, Inc. I'm an author, editor, and professional speaker.

How long have you been in business?

Eleven years.

Why did you choose this business?

My background is in communications, and I have a passion for encouraging others to live up to their full potential. Those two facets of my life come together nicely as I specialize in communicating—and encouraging—through the written and spoken word. Plus, I can work in my pajamas occasionally!

What's the toughest part of running a business and a family under one roof?

It's tough to find long, uninterrupted periods to work, especially during the summer. Plus, I'm constantly multitasking, which makes it difficult to focus my thoughts for the creative work I do. Finally, I have to be a jack of all trades. I'm my own administrative assistant, my own bookkeeper, my own technology guru, and my own janitor. Since it's not possible to be good at all of these things, I'm learning to surround myself with knowledgeable consultants who can help when I'm stuck.

What unique child care strategies have you used to enable you to work successfully from home?

When my children were young, we used to play "office" and all head to work together. Often I could get an extra hour's worth of work done while my kids played on our second computer, "filed," or wrote or illustrated their own books, which consisted of paper stapled together. My best strategy is still paying them to play quietly with one another. Their fee started at $1 per hour when they were young, and they've worked their way up since then. It's less expensive than many alternatives—and we're all still under the same roof!

What's your favorite part of being in business for yourself?

I love the freedom and flexibility. I enjoy getting paid to do work I love. And I appreciate the fact that I have so much control over what I do and who I do it with.

What's your least favorite part?

My work tends to be seasonal so I'm either very busy or wondering where my next paycheck is coming from. It would be nice to have a more steady rhythm, but after a decade, I've given up hoping for that!

What do you know now that you wish you would have known when you started?

I wish I would have known that I'd still be at it eleven years after I started. I believe that knowledge would have settled me down and made me feel less urgency about being successful right away. I still have to remind myself at times that I'm in this for the long haul and that I don't have to accomplish everything I want to right now.

What's the biggest mistake you've made as an at-home business owner?

Trying to minimize the impact on my family by making my work invisible. It caused a lot of unnecessary stress.

What's the smartest move you've made as an at-home business owner?

Instead of continuing to think I have to do everything myself, I've made a conscious effort to partner with individuals I believe can help me move my business forward more quickly than I could on my own. It costs money to do so, but instead of viewing it as an expense, I look at it as an investment.

What advice would you give to another woman who is interested in starting her own work-at-home business?

First, and most important, recognize that your children are only young once. I regret allowing myself to think some early opportunities would never come again if I didn't jump on them. Now I know that there is plenty of work, and I don't have to do it all right now. Second, be methodical in how you run your business. The more systems you have in place, the less stressful it will be. Third, be honest about the fact that you work from home. It doesn't do anyone any good to hide this fact. Fourth, recognize that a home-based business is a privilege. Many women would like to have one, but not all can. Finally, laugh when you can and be sure to give yourself plenty of days off!

2

why are you working?

understanding your motivation

It's a simple question, but the answer holds power when it comes to saving your sanity and mastering your business instead of letting it master you.

Why are you working?

Take some time to answer this question. If you keep a journal, open it up and write the question at the top of a blank page. Then capture everything that comes to mind.

Understanding the reason (or reasons) you work is essential to preserving your profit and saving your sanity. If you work to put food on the table or pay the mortgage, it makes sense to stay up late filling orders or to push yourself to make one more phone call even though your daughter is waking up from her nap. But if you're working for the fun of it or because you like the discounts you get on the products you sell, it may not be necessary to push yourself so hard each day. Understanding your motivation will help you master your business and keep it from mastering you.

When I asked the online group why they work, the majority of them said:

- My family depends on my income.
- I'm working for the "extras."
- I like the mental stimulation.
- I want to keep up with my industry/profession.
- I enjoy working.

Others noted:

- I love my children, but I need breaks from them.
- I am trying to build this business to a point where my husband can stay home as well. He currently has a job with a one- to two-hour commute.
- I want to meet new people.
- Right now it is a therapeutic outlet after the death of my father.
- I want to be available for my kids.
- I feel pressure from my husband.

Though your "why" may be different than those above, it's no less important.

Some people go through life without understanding why they work. In doing so, they miss the opportunity to be ful-filled. Don't be one of these people. When you know the answer to the "why" ques-tion, many other things will fall into place for you.

Understanding your motivation will help you master your business and keep it from mastering you.

As you're considering the "why" question, keep in mind that your answer may change over the life of your business. When I started working from home, my husband was employed by a large corporation. I began working for the mental stimulation and the opportunity to contribute a little to the family income. (And trust me, at the beginning it was very little!)

Since then, my husband has taken an early retirement package and is working under a contract that may end soon. Because the future is uncertain, it makes sense for me to maximize the opportunities that come my way. Not at the expense of my family, mind you, but I notice I'm willing to push just a little harder to ensure I have a continuous flow of work, something that wasn't as important to me several years ago when my children were preschool aged. As my "why" for working has evolved, so has my approach to business.

Your answer to the "why" question is important because it influences your motivation, your attitude, and your philosophy. Are you working toward a short-term goal? Are you hoping to build your business for long-term success? Are you just giving it a try to see what happens? All are valid reasons. Knowing your purpose for working is essential for one simple reason: your answer will help you make necessary business decisions in a way that reflects your values and desire to balance work and family.

If your goal is to "give it a try and see what happens," you may not need to arrange for regular child care or want to invest in costly computer software. If your goal is to earn just enough for a family vacation, you may simply decide to work hard during the spring and fall months and take most of the summers off to be with your kids. If, on the other hand, you plan to build a business that will sustain you for many years to come, you'll need to develop a long-term plan as well as a broad base of customers and clients.

Different motivations lead to different strategies. If you know the answer to the question "why am I working?" it will be easier for you to understand what your business needs are and what you'll have to do to achieve your goals.

When I first started working from home, I was happy to do a presentation and come home. I offered a half-dozen training programs and focused on those. Since my goal was simply to provide a few extras for my family, I didn't think about repeat business or developing additional programs so that I would have something to offer when a client invited me back for a return engagement.

As my "why" changed from helping with the "extras" for our family to developing a business that could help provide income for groceries, orthodontics, college, and retirement savings, I realized it would benefit me to develop new programs to help meet the needs I was hearing clients verbalize. Doing so has enabled me to develop long-term relationships rather than doing one presentation and leaving, and these long-term relationships have helped grow my business.

Paying attention to my answer to the "why" question also helped me realize that I needed to develop ways to earn income between speaking engagements. Writing and editing has been a great answer for me since it's something I can do from my home office.

How did you answer the "why" question—and how will the answer impact your work? Your reason should help you more easily determine the answers to the following questions:

- How much time do you need to spend each day or week working? (Perhaps you need to set regular "office hours" so that you can meet this commitment.)
- Does your work require a commitment from the whole family or can you squeeze it in early in the morning, late in the evening, or around naptime? And if you squeeze it in, how will it impact your family and your relationship with each member individually? (We'll address this issue more fully in the chapter on setting boundaries.)
- If your work requires you to invest time outside the home, when is the best time for this to happen?
- Are you willing to limit your business if it grows too quickly? If not, do you have people you can call on for help?

- Is your husband supportive of your business or does he just tolerate what you're doing? (Tolerance, as opposed to full support, can be stressful for the entire family.)
- If travel is required, how will you manage it?
- If you work outside the home in addition to your work at home, how much time are you realistically able to spend on your own business each week?

When you know why you are working, the answers to questions such as those above will be easier to discover. Let me give you an example.

Since my motivation is to contribute to our family income *while* being available to my children, I understand that it's simply not possible to accept every opportunity that comes my way without getting out of balance and meeting myself coming and going. As a result, I choose to limit the number of out-of-town speaking engagements I accept. Currently my limit is two per month so that I'm home far more than I'm gone. Occasionally, however, I'll accept additional opportunities after careful consideration. (After all, more engagements means a little more in the college fund!)

Though it's difficult to turn down business to remain committed to my priorities, I understand that it's necessary. Understanding why you work will help you when it comes to scheduling your work and home life as well. In fact, the ability to place limitations on ourselves as entrepreneurs may be one of the most important skills we develop in mastering our business so that it doesn't master us.

Whether you're a piano teacher, a tutor, a sales representative, or a graphic artist, it's essential that you know why you are working. When you do, you'll find it's easier to determine what your schedule should look like, how hard you need to work, and what type of limitations you may need to place on yourself so that you don't become a workaholic or neglect the reason you are home to begin with: your family. Understanding "why" will help you answer every other question you'll face: who, what, when, where, and how.

Even if you've been in business for years, it's helpful to take time to answer the "why" question. Maybe the answer is the same as it was when you began working at home. Or maybe it has changed. Either way, understanding why you're doing what you're doing will help you decide how to do it in a way that allows you to live a balanced and sane life. And if you know the answer to the question but your life isn't balanced or sane, turn to the next chapter to discover the second question every successful at-home entrepreneur must answer.

Lesson Learned: Understanding why you're working will help you discover answers to all the other questions you must ask as a business owner, including how to keep your personal and professional lives in balance even though they coexist under one roof.

3

how much is enough?

identifying your goals

Understanding why you're working is the first step to profit and sanity in a home-based business. But there's a second question you must also ask: *how much monetary profit is enough?* By this I mean, what's the minimum amount you need or want to make this year in your business?

At first my answer to that question was simply, "As much as possible." But making "as much as possible" required me to work "as much as possible." With two young children underfoot, that meant stealing away to my office whenever I could—even at the expense of exercise, sleep, and most sadly, my marital relationship.

I acted like a junkie looking for her next hit. My drug of choice was free minutes during which I could check email or make a phone call. "Let's see," I'd think, "the kids will go down for a nap in an hour, and then I can get some work done." Instead of living in the moment, I spent a year counting them so I could get to my next work session. I know that I missed opportunities to snuggle and read books out loud and collect worms and play hopscotch. But I was making "as much as possible."

Eventually "as much as possible" led to such strain on my marriage that my husband and I became two ships passing in the night, barely acknowledging each other. It seemed every sentence I spoke started with the words, "I need a little time to work. Would you mind watching the kids?" Resentment began to build. I resented the fact that my work came second to his (even though his salary at the time was much higher and provided our family health benefits), and he resented the fact that all I could think about was work.

I was earning "as much as possible," but it took a physical and mental toll on me. It affected my family relationships. It overwhelmed me. Until I asked, "How much is enough?"

Honestly, I'm not sure where the question came from. I just remember writing these words in my journal one day: *What does success look like for me in my business, and when will I know I've achieved it?*

While the question flowed easily from my pen, the answer stumped me. As I stared at the page, I thought about "success." As I contemplated the concept, I realized that money was a very small part of it for me. I did not want to have money but no one to share it with. Nor did I want to have money but be too tired or ill to spend it. As I pondered the question, I realized that "as much as possible" was a bottomless pit. There would always be more money to make or more work to do. By striving for "as much as possible," I was sentencing myself to a life of endless work. Though I claimed my family was important, "as much as possible" had taken over. Something had to give.

That's when I decided to put pen to paper to answer the question "How much is enough?"

I started by listing the family expenses I hoped to cover with my profit. Then I identified the goals I'd like to help save for, including a family vacation, college tuition, and retirement. I added these amounts together. The resulting number, plus my average overhead expense, became my "how much."

To further understand my goal, I divided by twelve to get an idea of how much I wanted to make each month. The number seemed doable. In fact, it was less scary than "as much as possible" because it was a finite number. Now, using my computer software, I can tell at any point in the year if I'm close to my goal. If not, I may make another phone call or two. If I'm ahead of my goal, I relax.

> Focusing on "enough" as opposed to "as much as possible" has enabled me to find peace as an entrepreneur.

Knowing how much is enough allows me to operate from a position of strength rather than constantly struggling to make "as much as possible." The frantic urgency I once felt has given way to a welcome rhythm in my work. Some of this may be the result of having been in business for over a decade and having the historical perspective that I do. But I can't help but think that focusing on the "enough" part—rather than worrying about amassing and hoarding money—has also settled me. "Enough" speaks to the idea that there is plenty to go around and that I won't be lacking, even if I'm not rolling in dough. It says that I'll have "enough" even when my schedule is empty and I don't have any prospects for future work, and that I will be able to help provide for my children even if my circumstances change.

Focusing on "enough" as opposed to "as much as possible" has enabled me to find peace as an entrepreneur. Rather than operating from a place of worry, I trust that there will be work in the future. Instead of guarding what I have, I feel free to share with those less fortunate. And rather than feeling totally responsible for what happens in my business, I'm able to recognize God's provision, knowing that all I am and have come from him to begin with.

A seismic internal shift occurred when "as much as possible" gave way to focusing instead on "enough." No longer do I have to worry about constantly striving to make another dollar. Instead,

I can do my work and do it well, focused simply on meeting my goal for the year.

My goal is a measuring stick that helps me know when I need to work a little harder and makes it easier for me to periodically relax or turn down work. By naming "enough" with a dollar figure, I give myself permission to pursue profit but not at the expense of my relationships. I choose to work toward "enough" but not to pursue "as much as possible." I work hard but schedule time for play. I'm faithful to my work-related to-do list but make sure that things like exercise and volunteering are on the list as well. I put my nose to the grindstone while simultaneously taming my ambition so that work doesn't become my life.

Naming "enough" for yourself will give you something to work toward. It addresses the profit issue. If you set a realistic goal, it also addresses the sanity issue. You'll work but not work around the clock. You'll earn but won't fall prey to the tyranny of earning "as much as possible." You'll benefit financially but won't sacrifice your relationships to do so.

Oddly, when I began focusing on "enough" rather than "as much as possible," I began to make more money. Knowing how much is enough made it possible for me to work smarter, not harder, and to identify what is most profitable for me. It released me from charging after "as much as possible" and enabled me to more easily figure out what I needed to do to earn "enough." The difference in my life and business has been staggering.

> Determining how much is enough enabled me to control my business instead of letting it control me.

Now I control my business instead of letting it control me—all because I took the time to understand why I'm working and how much is enough, two key questions for at-home CEOs.

How much is enough for you? It's worth taking the time to answer the question. Like the answer to *"Why are you working?"* your response to *"How much is enough?"* has great power to positively affect your business decisions and influence your actions.

Will you work on weekends? It depends on why you're working and how much is enough. Will you work full time or part time? It depends on why you're working and how much is enough. How heavily will you invest in your business? It depends on why you're working and how much is enough. Do you need regular child care? It depends on why you're working and how much is enough.

Understanding your motivation and your goals makes it easier to figure out what it will take to meet them. It also makes it easier not to let your business rule you. Instead of operating from fear and lack, you'll operate from a position of strength and abundance—a powerful place for at-home entrepreneurs and the families they love.

Lesson Learned: Figuring out how much is enough and focusing on it, as opposed to making "as much as possible," will enable you to find balance and peace as both a mom and an entrepreneur.

Work-at-Home Mom Profile

Amy Bifano

Name and type of business:
Piece O'Cake. Cake decorating, specifically wedding cakes.

How long have you been in business?
Seven years.

Why did you choose this business?
Baking is a passion of mine, and I think the business chose me instead of the other way around! I started off by doing friends' birthday cakes as favors, and then those folks started referring me to other people. Before I knew it, I was making money instead of doing it only for fun!

What's the toughest part of running a business and a family under one roof?
Two things: the office is never closed, and clients call me at all hours of the day. Also, my office is our kitchen, and things get a little crazy when I am busy with cakes.

What unique child care strategies have you used to enable you to work successfully from home?
When my kids were younger, I tried to work while they were sleeping or at preschool or school. Now that they are older, I actually try to involve them in my business. Sometimes my daughter will come with me on appointments and will discuss some of her favorite wedding cakes with my brides. She came to her first appointment when she was four years old (my child care had fallen through) and when we were done, she asked me why the bride didn't have her dress on! Helping me gives her a little bit of ownership and pride, and the brides always like her. I think she is a selling tool! My kids also go with me to deliver cakes and set them up. They are quick to offer me their thoughts and suggestions.

What's your favorite part of being in business for yourself?
The flexibility it offers. I can schedule things around my family's schedule. I very rarely miss important school functions or other events. And my husband and I can go on lunch dates.

What's your least favorite part?
I have no routine. Every day is different, and sometimes it is hard to stay focused. There are times when I will put things off because "something" comes up. Then

things pile up, and the workload becomes bigger than I like it to be. It is easy to get distracted because you know the workload only affects you. Family emergencies are another challenge. When my father was ill and eventually passed away, I had several weddings during that time. I had made a commitment to those brides, and they were depending upon me for their special day. It added a lot of stress to an already stressful time to try to be there for my dad and also not disappoint those brides.

What do you know now that you wish you would have known when you started?

How quickly things can spiral out of control and you don't know until you are in the middle of it! I used to get so excited taking on new customers and making that special cake for them, but it took its toll on me and my family when it came time to do the work. My daughter even told me on more than one occasion, "You like your cakes more than you like me!" That hurt and served as a wake-up call for me that I was being a little too aggressive about taking on new clients. I also did not start out with a business plan, which would have helped.

What's the biggest mistake you've made as an at-home business owner?

I wasn't very smart about the "business" side of things. Baking is my passion, and I didn't like associating that with making money. I'm still not sure I do, but my husband likes it when I bring in the money! To be honest, I probably don't charge enough for my services. Many times I think I am not a "professional" because I work out of my house and therefore cannot charge what other commercial bakers might charge.

What's the smartest move you've made as an at-home business owner?

It helped tremendously when I went from doing all sorts of decorated cakes to focusing mainly on wedding cakes. This enabled me to plan ahead more easily and simplified my business.

What's the most mortifying "mom moment" you've had in running your at-home business?

I had a client show up unexpectedly at my house when it was a disaster. I'm sure the bride was thinking, "She is going to bake my cake in this mess?" And of course, there's always the moment when you are on the phone and your kids are fighting with each other in the background!

What advice would you give to another woman who is interested in starting her own work-at-home business?

Set aside "business hours" and make sure you figure out how much business you want before it escalates and becomes too big. Know what your goals are. I wanted to provide some extra income for my family but still remain a "stay-at-home mom" as my top priority. Without having that goal in mind, my business could easily escalate into opening a shop and going on from there!

4

"i can't work in these conditions!"

setting boundaries

The phone rang. I balanced my son in my arms as I picked up the receiver and said hello. Though I was in my pajamas with Play-Doh strewn around me, the caller had no idea. Just to make sure, I used my best business voice when I answered.

It was a vice president calling. He was in charge of finding a speaker for an upcoming meeting. I grabbed the back of the grocery list and jotted down the details. The date. The time. The location. The goals for the program. As he spoke, my son started to fuss. So I did what any enterprising lactating work-from-home mom would do: I pulled up my shirt and offered my son my breast. He ate contentedly while I negotiated a deal, acting all along as if this was the most natural thing in the world, even though I knew it wasn't.

As I continued to jot down notes, I noticed it was quiet. *Where is my daughter?* I wondered as I wrote. Pen in hand, baby in arms, I turned to scan the room. She sat happily, keeping herself busy— drawing on the kitchen walls with her markers.

My heart skipped a beat as I saw the artwork. I knew I should excuse myself from the call and rescue the walls. But she was quiet, and a quick look at the markers assured me they were washable. The call was almost over. I let her continue to draw, despite the fact that my blood pressure was elevating with every passing second. I remember thinking at the time, *Desperate times make desperate mothers.* And I was indeed desperate. Trying to juggle work and family was tapping every ounce of creativity and patience I possessed.

Looking back, I wonder why I even bothered to pick up the phone with both children awake and needy. But I know that at the time I was afraid I'd lose business if I didn't answer every call.

Now I think I was off my rocker to breastfeed while on the phone. Then I tricked myself into believing that callers couldn't hear what was happening in the background as we spoke. (I blush now thinking of my naiveté!)

Now I'm appalled that I actually let my daughter produce a mural on the wall while I stood just steps away. Then I felt for certain that if I didn't book that engagement, I'd never book another one.

As I hung up the phone, I half expected Allen Funt from *Candid Camera* to appear from around the corner and shout "Surprise!" Instead of Allen Funt, I'm the one who shouted. "I can't work in these conditions!" I hollered. Then I started to cry.

As tears spilled down my cheeks, my daughter apologized for drawing on the wall and tried to comfort me, thinking that her actions alone were responsible for my sadness. I accepted the apology, laid my son down in his crib, and then proceeded to wash the walls. I'm sure I lectured her—but internally I also lectured myself. Was I so desperate to work that I couldn't even show some restraint in choosing when to conduct business? Was the middle of playtime really the best time to pick up the phone? How had the line between work and home blurred so much that I was breastfeeding while booking an engagement?

As I chided myself, I realized that prior to that moment I thought necessity required that I be available for business at any and all times. Until then I thought I had no choice in regard to when or how much I worked. As I washed the walls, however, I began to wonder what would happen if I ran my business proactively instead of letting it run me and if limits would really limit me—or if they'd free me instead. I decided to experiment and find out.

What I learned was simple: limits didn't limit me after all. In fact, they made me more effective as I focused more fully on what was most profitable and intentionally decided to let some opportunities pass me by. Setting boundaries actually made me more profitable, not less.

These are some of the boundaries I found helpful and continue to subscribe to:

- I only answer the phone if the kids are settled and I'm confident I can complete a phone call without distraction or interruption.

- I conduct as much business as possible via email and am proactive about making telephone appointments so that I know I'll be alone and focused when doing my most important work. I prefer to schedule morning conference calls so that my children are in school and away from my office while I'm on the phone.

- I try to group personal appointments and errands one or two days a week so that I have large blocks of uninterrupted time for work the remaining days of the week.

- I choose not to give out my cell phone number routinely so I can use it for my own ease instead of clients' convenience.

- When the kids are off school for a day, I sometimes hire a sitter to come to our house to keep them occupied in the morning or arrange for them to go to their grandma's so that I can work. Then I make myself available to them in the afternoon.

- When additional work is necessary, I try to schedule it for Saturday mornings so that I'm not hidden in my office on school nights when the kids may need me.

- When travel is required, I try to get to and from an engagement as quickly as possible, minimizing the time I'm away. I also try not to make plans for the night before I leave or the evening I return so that I'm fully available to my family immediately prior to leaving and upon my return.

- I've learned to negotiate deadlines when I'm overloaded instead of simply adding more work when I'm least able to handle it. If I'm not able to negotiate a favorable deadline, I turn down the work. (This was scary at first but has gotten less scary as the years roll by.)

The day I realized I could no longer "work in these conditions" with young children underfoot was the day I changed the stressful conditions (many of which I unknowingly created myself) using the boundaries above. I'm still flummoxed at how it is possible to limit your business while simultaneously growing it, but I'm not the only one who has experienced this sanity-saving concept.

Tim Ferriss, author of *The Four-Hour Work Week*, also discovered the power of limits. In 2004 he had 120 wholesale customers worldwide. He began his day at 7:00 a.m. and worked until 9:00 p.m., starting with phone calls to the United Kingdom and ending with calls to Asia and Australia. After deciding he no longer wanted to work such long days, he carefully analyzed his customer base and realized that five of his 120 customers were contributing more than 90 percent of his profit! During an audio interview, Ferriss noted, "They required no maintenance, they simply placed reorders. They were the easiest to deal with."

That realization led him to acknowledge that five very profitable customers meant he also had 115 minimally productive, high-maintenance customers. So what did he do? He says, "I put all of those 115 on auto-pilot. They could place orders, but I wouldn't call them to see how they were doing." Instead, he chose to focus on cultivating his five most profitable customers as well as profiling and duplicating them.

> If you're struggling to balance work and family, consider placing limits on your work that will help you meet the needs of both your business and your family without sacrificing either one.

The results? Ferriss says, "I increased profit by about 50 percent within two or three months, and at the same time, my management time for all those wholesalers dropped from about 60 hours per week to less than two hours per week."[1]

While it's unlikely that you and I could produce such spectacular gains, our sanity depends on learning from this example. Boundaries don't necessarily limit your business. Instead, they make your work life more pleasant and enjoyable and may, in fact, also make you more profitable.

If you're struggling to balance work and family, consider placing limits on your work that will help you meet the needs of both your business and your family without sacrificing either one. Here are some questions to get you started:

- What's the minimum number of hours I need to work each week to ensure my business will thrive?
- How many parties or demonstrations do I need to book each week or month in order to meet my sales goals—and how many are comfortable for my family?
- When is the best time for me to work, based on our family schedule?
- How can family members support my business (stuffing bags, filing, babysitting, filling orders, etc.) so that they feel a part of it?
- Will I provide a cell phone number for clients and customers, and if so, am I really willing to be on call at all times?

- What can I do to help ensure a steady work pace so that it's not feast or famine?
- Is seasonal work preferable for me because it allows me to work hard for short periods followed by resting space for my family?
- Are the current ages of my children conducive to the type of business I'm running?
- How can I use technology to streamline my workload?

While it may seem elementary to consider the questions above, it was revolutionary for me due to my fear. I feared that if I wasn't always available, I'd lose business. I feared that if I didn't always say yes when a client called, they'd never call again. And I feared that if I wasn't immediately successful, I'd never be. None of these fears proved true. But I had to set boundaries to find that out.

What kinds of fears are limiting you in your business? The fear of not making a profit? The fear of not meeting sales goals or booking enough parties? The fear that you won't be able to sustain your current success? If your business is young, these fears are natural. But if your business is seasoned, take a look at your history so that your fears are either founded on truth or dispelled altogether. It's been helpful for me to be able to look back over a decade and see that somehow I've managed to make it despite both lean and lush times. Instead of keeping an insane schedule and working insane hours, I know I can limit my business and still be profitable.

What boundaries will help you stay sane and allow you to meet family needs as well? It's a question worth asking and answering for yourself as well as those you love. The sooner you do this, the better.

Lesson Learned: Boundaries don't necessarily limit your business. They may, in fact, help you become both more sane and more profitable.

5

guilt

the at-home entrepreneur's worst enemy

"I always feel I am letting someone down."

"I feel guilty not being able to just sit with my kids and play or watch TV when they are home."

"I feel guilty when I get frustrated at the kids because I feel they are 'in my way' when I need to get business things done."

"I feel as though my life is one big melting pot where my home, work, and personal life are combined in one big huge bucket and I can't separate anything out."

"I work at home so I can be here with my children, but it feels like I am constantly putting them off, so I don't always feel like I am accomplishing the goal of being there for them."

These are quotes from real moms.

Whether working at home or not, every mom wrestles with guilt. Work-at-home moms have a different kind of guilt: sometimes our body is at home but our mind is not.

By definition, guilt is "a feeling of responsibility or remorse for some offense, crime, wrong, etc., whether real or imagined." I believe that it's "the feeling of responsibility" that leads to so much guilt. We're responsible for our children's health and well-being, their education, their manners, and their spiritual growth and development. We want them to grow up to be considerate, responsible citizens, and we feel the need to protect them from all the evil in the world, to a name a few of the more pressing mom concerns. And that's just the beginning of the list!

No wonder we feel guilty. When we become parents, we accept a huge level of responsibility, and though we do our best, it's just not possible to do it perfectly. Thus, the guilt. Add a home-based business and there's even more to feel guilty about.

> Unhealthy guilt serves no purpose.

I've wrestled with all kinds of guilt as a mom, but none has been more troubling than the work-at-home guilt I feel, similar to that expressed by the women quoted at the beginning of this chapter. Without clear delineation between work and home, it's especially easy to feel like you're barely treading water and not doing anything well, leading to work-at-home mom guilt.

Healthy guilt is designed to keep you from doing something you shouldn't. Healthy guilt leads to remorse and moves you to some apologetic action. Unhealthy guilt serves no purpose. As work-at-home moms, we need to discern the difference. Our challenge is to refuse to let unhealthy, unearned, or false guilt take root in our lives.

Feeling guilty doesn't change a thing. It just makes you feel lousy. When you feel guilty, take time to examine why. If there is a legitimate reason for the guilt, do something about it. If not, refuse to continue to harbor this nasty emotion. When I feel guilty for no good reason, I allow myself to wallow in the feeling for three minutes, and then I force myself to move on. It's a powerful exercise that has enabled me to move from confusion to confidence as a work-at-home mom.

As you work to determine whether your guilt is warranted or not, take a look at your home-work balance as well as why you work the way you do. If you're a workaholic, if you're working to avoid someone or something in your family, or if you actually prefer work to being with your family, there may well be an underlying issue that needs your attention. When I first started working at home, work was how I measured my self-worth as opposed to being "just a mom." Now I see how shallow that was. But because I measured myself by the work, the transition home was difficult for me. Looking back, I recognize how I clung to what I had previously known in the workplace instead of developing a new definition of success. It's taken me years to yield to a new pattern of thinking.

If you're struggling with guilt, here's how to handle it:

Develop clear policies designed to help you keep work and home separate as much as possible. With no clear delineation between work and family time, you may feel like you're working 24/7. And if you're constantly searching for a few free minutes to work, like I did, you may, in fact, be working around the clock. This isn't healthy, and it's frustrating for family members. It's been much more effective for me to set regular office hours and to abide by them as much as possible. (This is obviously easier if your children are older.) Kids become less frustrated if they know mommy is going to work until lunchtime and then be free to play with them or that she will be in her office during their nap time but will take them to the park after they rest.

Teach your children how to respect your work time. One woman I know taught her children to "Stop, look, and listen" before entering her office. They were to stop on the threshold of her office, look to see what she was doing, listen to see if she was on the phone, and enter only if she was not. She taught them to enter quietly and stand next to her until she reached a stopping point in her work. Then she would turn her full attention to them. (Obviously her children were past the toddler stage when she did this.) By teaching her children to respect her work and by respecting their needs when they entered her office, she was able to develop a peaceful coexistence for work and family in her home and reduce the guilt she felt trying to balance the two.

I also read about a mom who cut out a red traffic stop sign and held it up when her children entered her office while she was on the phone. It was a visual reminder for the kids and a way for her to communicate with them nonverbally when she needed their attention. Often I've snapped my fingers to get my kids' attention when they were being too loud while I was on the phone. And yes, I've given them the universal "hand slashing the throat" signal more than once to get them to stop what they were doing. It's not my favorite way to communicate, but they know I mean business if I have to resort to that gesture!

I finally got smart and invested in distinctive ringing for my work phone number. For just a few extra dollars per month, we have two different numbers on one phone line. When a business call comes in, we hear two short rings consecutively rather than the long ring of our home number. My children know they have to be quiet when they hear the double ring. I only pick up the phone if everyone is settled and I actually have time to talk. Otherwise, I let it roll over to voice mail.

I wasn't always so smart, nor my children as cooperative. Once, when I was on the phone, my son was behaving terribly. Instead of excusing myself from the call and returning it later, which would have been much smarter, I simply covered the handset and, thinking the caller couldn't hear, said to my son, "You are in BIG trouble. Go to your room NOW!" When I got back on the line, the man on the other end said, "What did he do?" You can imagine my humiliation and embarrassment! I've talked to lots of work-at-home moms who have their own humbling phone stories, including the mom whose son yelled, "I have to go poop and I have to go now!" so loudly that all six people on her conference call heard it.

I suggest never using a phone that doesn't have a mute button on it. You owe it to yourself, your children, and your clients. It's money well spent. And remember, you can write it off as a business expense, along with the headset that will allow you to fold clothes while you're talking to a long-winded client.

Include your children in your work when you are able. Including your children in your work makes them feel important. I started by asking my kids to help assemble and staple handouts (which sometimes had to be redone when they weren't looking). Last week I asked my daughter to assist me at my book table for the first time. She did a beautiful job. And even though I told her she could read quietly in the back of the room while I spoke, she told me afterward that she didn't read at all but listened to my entire program! I was deeply touched and realized how valuable it was for her to see what I do when I'm away from home. If there's a way to show your kids what you do, it's beneficial for them, as long as they can observe you without being a distraction or calling your professionalism into question.

Be sure that the work you ask your children to do is age appropriate. If they help you fill orders, spot check their work. In addition, it's wise to match the work they do with their attention span. I've found that my kids lose interest after twenty or thirty minutes. Consequently, I try to limit my invitations to quick jobs such as photocopying or helping load the car.

If your children help you on a regular basis, consider paying them. According to June Walker, a tax adviser:

> The wages are taxable to your child at her tax bracket, not yours. You reduce your profit by paying out a wage expense, and if your child is under eighteen, you will pay no Social Security or federal unemployment taxes on her wages (often no state payroll taxes

either). Your child must have a real job (not $200 per week to empty waste paper baskets). You will also have to file all payroll forms, but the additional paperwork and cost is usually worth it. (Note: when your child's tax return is prepared, there are special rules if she is under fourteen and has investment income.)[1]

Recognize the value of your work in contributing to your family income, modeling a work ethic, and preparing your children for their own work someday. The reality is that for many families, it takes two wage earners to make ends meet. I know that we could survive without me working, but I also know things would be *very* different for our family if we did. We've chosen the path that enables us to meet our financial commitments and goals (including saving for college and retirement) most comfortably. That choice comes with a price, however, and that price is that sometimes I have to work instead of doing whatever I want or being available for activities. That's adulthood for you! And it's a lesson our children need to learn as well: growing up comes with responsibilities.

One advantage of working from home is that my kids see how hard I work. They see the discipline required to report to my desk day after day as I develop a manuscript. They hear about the hassles of travel, including long security lines and delayed and cancelled flights. They've watched me carry my books from our downstairs storage room and load them into the back of the van for a speaking engagement. Sometimes they watch me carry them back again. They know that work is called work for a reason.

As I model a work ethic for my children, I'm also careful to let them see the rewards. It's currently spring break, and tomorrow I'm taking the day off for a road trip with them. As we pull out of the driveway, I'll thank them for the times they've been quiet or kept themselves busy this week so that I could work, and I'll let them know that it's part of my proceeds that make that day possible. I'm always careful to remind them how hard their dad works too and to acknowledge the part he plays in making an outing like this possible. By focusing on the fun we'll have tomorrow, I've been able to feel less guilty today. And by sprinkling fun in with periods of work, children learn about the give and take of life.

Consider the alternative. When guilt begins to consume me because I'm writing while my kids watch TV or I'm emailing while they are throwing water balloons in the backyard, I consider the alternative. If I didn't work from home, they'd be somewhere else with someone else and I wouldn't even know what they were doing. Though we may be in different rooms, I'm usually just a few steps away. I prepare their meals; I monitor their movements. This is not an indictment of moms who work outside the home. Instead, it's gratitude for this season of my mothering life and the flexibility I currently have. The arrangement may not be perfect, but there are many good things about it. I choose to focus on these when I begin to feel guilty.

Mix it up. In the Bible, Ecclesiastes 3:1 says, "There is a time for everything, and a season for every activity under heaven." I think it's valuable for work-at-home moms to fully embrace this. There is a time to labor and a time for play. A time for profit and a time to nurture. The challenge is figuring out what needs to happen when. It's not easy. As one mom shared, "When I work hard enough to make good money and pay the bills with maybe some left over, then I compromise time with the family. When I spend more time with the family, there doesn't seem to be enough money. It's a catch-22."

I feel less guilty when I'm able to create time for everything. Time for clients and time for kids. Time for bookkeeping and time for reading books to my kids. Time for playing phone tag and time for playing tag in the backyard.

By mixing it up, I'm more able to make time for everything. As a work-at-home mom, I don't move out of the house at 8:00 in the morning and return at 5:00 at night like many women. Instead, I move in and out of my kids' space throughout the day. It's this moving out and moving in repeatedly—instead of moving out, staying out for the workday, and then moving back in—that makes at-home work and mothering simultaneously difficult and rewarding. I can interact and monitor in ways that other women can't. And yet I still have work to do that calls me like a siren from the deep.

Arlene Rossen Cardozo speaks to the challenge of varying one's pace as a mother and CEO. In her book *Sequencing* she quotes a mother who tried to return to part-time work outside the home when her child was two years old. The mom wrote, "I found how different the rhythm of being in a workplace is from being with children. The more hours I worked away from home, the more convinced I became that trying to make both these rhythms work every day was a monumental task."[2] Eventually this mom left the workplace altogether.

I've tried to explain this rhythm issue to family and friends. Most stare at me uncomprehendingly. But when I talk to other work-at-home moms about the dissonance that comes with operating a home and business under one roof, they immediately understand how difficult it is to pick up the pace for a conference call or sales demonstration after lollygagging in the sunshine. One mom shared, "Life and motherhood just keep getting in the way, and my office does not have a door I can close (and lock). It is in the front room of our farmhouse, and so the daily noises, and kids, keep coming in." Another wrote, "Sometimes you just have to stop what you're doing and pay attention to the kids. This morning, even though I had work to do, my daughter and I played in shaving cream on the kitchen table."

These women accept the challenge of moving back and forth between work and family because they've lived it. And they recognize that sometimes it's just easier to call it quits for the day than to continue a frantic work pace when your children require you to slow down and shift gears.

The key is having your priorities in order and having enough self-discipline to work as much as you need to but no more. It's a battle I face every day. I'm resigned to the fact that as long as I'm living and working under one roof with children, the battle won't end. But after years of letting guilt hang around my neck and weigh me down, I refuse to keep its company any longer—unless it keeps me from doing something I shouldn't. Any other guilt gets three minutes of attention and then I move on. I'm doing what I'm doing to benefit my family. Feeling guilty about it just makes me less effective.

Perhaps cartoonist Cathy Guisewite summed it up best: "Food, love, career, and mothers, the four major guilt groups."

Guilt is part of being a mother. But it doesn't have to be part of your work-at-home routine if you follow the suggestions outlined in this chapter.

Lesson Learned: Guilt serves no purpose. File it under "U" for useless and don't let it take hold in your work-at-home life.

Work-at-Home Mom Profile

Kristin Maletich

Name and type of business:
Key Players Piano Studio. Private piano instruction.

How long have you been in business?
Twenty-three years.

Why did you choose this business?
It allowed me to do what I love (teaching) without leaving home. Initially, I began teaching private lessons because my oldest was a toddler and I was reluctant to leave her with a sitter in order to work part time outside of the home.

What's the toughest part of running a business and a family under one roof?
Probably trying to keep the house a "home" that belongs to the family while it is also a place of business with the public going in and out. Having a supportive husband is paramount, and mine was always really helpful. My children grew up with the business in the house, which made it easier for them because they always understood that it happened every day.

What unique child care strategies have you used to enable you to work successfully from home?
When my children were very young, I began teaching after my husband got home from work. He usually walked in the door with me there to hand him a child and go to work in the next room. Because my hours are after school, I have asked a high school student to help out on occasion. My sister, who lived across the street from me in the early days, had children older than mine (and younger than mine), so we took turns having the available "babysitter." We didn't plan that, but it sure did work out nicely!

What's your favorite part of being in business for yourself?
Being home when my children came home from school. Even though I was teaching, I was accessible to them. They never had to come home to an empty

house, and that was really important to me. I also have enjoyed being my own boss. Over the years it has enabled me to learn quite a lot.

What's your least favorite part?

The hours. I teach school-age children, so I can't begin my work hours until after they are done with their school day. I work into the evening instead of during the daytime. Otherwise it's the best job on the planet.

What do you know now that you wish you would have known when you started?

I wish I had known that I needed to keep everything very professional when I started. I began thinking I could accommodate everyone and ended up being taken advantage of on several occasions. Correcting that took work.

What's the biggest mistake you've made as an at-home-business owner?

Neglecting to have a list of "rules" (in writing) for my studio. After I began publishing a list of ground rules, everything got easier. It took three or four years to fully understand that.

What's the smartest move you've made as an at-home business owner?

Dedicating an actual studio portion of our home to the business. I began working in our living room, but having the business in a separate room of its own allows my family to feel less like the house is a business and more like it belongs to them.

What advice would you give to another woman who is interested in starting her own work-at-home business?

Begin small and make sure the business is going to work for you. Love what you are doing, because the juggling that you will need to do between work and family will be harder if you aren't happy with what you're doing. Start the business with a professional approach from the beginning and take your business seriously. Your commitment to your business leads others to respect your working from home. Also make sure your family is on board with your idea. Having a home business is ten times easier if everyone understands what it will require and is supportive.

6

the parental pact

creating the perfect team

I wish I had known how much strain running a home-based business would place on my marriage. If I had, perhaps I wouldn't have ignored the stress as long as I did or refused to accept the fact that I might be responsible for it.

Prior to launching my at-home business, my husband Stuart and I both worked outside the home. When our daughter came along, she was cared for by a woman from my church who had an in-home day care. I dropped her off in the mornings, and my husband picked her up after work so that I could head straight home and start dinner.

When we decided I would take a hiatus to care for the children, home became my responsibility and work became his. These assignments worked—until I began freelancing and the demands on my time increased.

Slowly my focus again became both home and work while my husband's remained solely on work. Somehow we didn't notice how the shift was affecting us. Nor did we renegotiate our individual roles as my workload increased. Resentment reared its ugly head.

Grateful for the flexibility offered by working from home, I didn't feel I should complain. As I shared in earlier chapters, I dutifully fit my work in around naptimes and household chores. I diligently kept up with the laundry, ensured the children were well cared for, coordinated the household schedule, and made it a priority to have a meal on the table the majority of the time, in addition to responding to client requests and demands. I tried to make my work as invisible as possible. Eventually, doing so required late nights and a lot of early mornings, which led to sleep deprivation and grumpiness on my part.

Many envied my life as an at-home entrepreneur, but most couldn't see that my boat was slowly sinking. So was my marriage.

My inability to say no to clients meant I was indirectly saying no to my family on a regular basis. My heightened stress level spilled over to our personal interactions and tainted our time together. My need to find significance in work made it difficult for me to stop and smell the roses with my family.

I was too nearsighted and stubborn to admit any of this. Now that time has passed, I can clearly see how my narrow focus had a negative impact on all of us, including me.

A war raged within me. I love to work, have the drive and ambition to do so, and am sufficiently skilled to contribute to the family income. I also love my family, care about their needs, and want the best for each member.

Though I had never spoken to my husband directly about it, I assumed he was on board with my profit-making motives and that he'd be glad to make his own sacrifices to help me reach my goals. Though I never gave him the chance to weigh in on the subject, I expected him to happily come home and work a second shift while I went to my office each evening to work my own second shift. I counted on him to relinquish Saturdays so that I could meet my deadlines. And I insisted I should have the freedom to work just like he did.

As the work piled up and stress mounted, the situation took its toll. One day I realized all I could think about was when I would next have uninterrupted time to work. I recognized this wasn't healthy for me or anyone in my family. I took a hard look at my assumptions and demands and realized I was completely out of balance. As a result, I began a dialogue with my husband and asked the questions I should have asked much sooner. These questions may be helpful for you as well:

- Are you willing to support me as I work from home?
- If so, what's realistic in terms of how much I work?
- Do you have a set amount of money you'd like for me to make? (If the number you and your husband have in mind is vastly different, don't proceed any further until you're able to come to an agreement on what's best for the two of you as a couple and for your family as a whole.)
- In what ways are you most comfortable supporting my work?
- Are there things I can do to more fully support you in your work too?
- May I count on you for extra help around the house? If not, are you comfortable with me hiring someone to help?
- What kind of limitations should we put in place to keep things balanced? (Consider limits on the number of shows or demonstrations you book in a week, the number of days you're willing to travel each month, or the number of weekend and evening hours you'll work.)
- Are there times of the year you'd like for me to limit my workload in order to not add stress to the family schedule or your own workload?
- What's the best way to approach one another if we feel things are shifting out of balance?

Managing work-life balance, even for those who don't work at home, requires constant communication and a willingness to make adjustments as necessary. It's just as essential for couples in which one or both individuals work at home. At our house, the lack of communication in the beginning led to marital disharmony that came from the feeling that we were on opposing teams rather than teammates reaching for the same goals.

If you have preschool-age children or children with special needs, are home-schooling, are married to a man who's

> Managing work-life balance requires constant communication and a willingness to make adjustments as necessary.

also self-employed, or have a large number of children, you need to know that the potential for stress resulting from lack of communication is even higher for you than it is for other parents. Young children challenge even the best marriages. Young children combined with one or more at-home entrepreneurs in the family can be combustible! Take note and heed this advice: *the tougher your work-at-home challenge, the more important the parental pact.*

Though I've been working from home for over a decade, it's just in the last couple of years that I've started to feel we're humming along on all cylinders as a family. Part of this is because my children are old enough to more fully participate in their own care, but part of it is because we finally have a family routine that's comfortable. I limit the amount of work I accept, negotiate deadlines when possible so I don't have multiple ones bearing down on me at once, and talk to my husband *before* I accept additional work if I know it means his schedule will be affected.

Common courtesy? Perhaps. But when you're an ambitious, high-achieving person, or an entrepreneur whose family is dependent on your income, sometimes it's hard to remember that your choices affect more than just you. And if you're stubborn like me (not one of my better attributes, mind you), sometimes you're unwilling to admit that you're the heartbeat of your family and need to curtail your activities to keep the beat steadily going.

Lesson Learned: The parental pact is an essential part of work-at-home success. Don't begin without one. Then continue to communicate honestly and consistently to ensure the pact remains strong and all parties are committed to making work at home work.

7

child care strategies for every season of your work-at-home life

I wrote part of my first book with a toddler on my lap and some of my second with a child standing behind me on my office chair running his fingers through my hair.

I've packed for overnight trips only to come out of the bathroom and find that while I was in the bathroom, my son unpacked my bag for me.

I've shown up for client meetings with childish scribbles defacing my meeting notes.

And I once bribed my kids with raisins and a later trip to McDonald's so they'd sit quietly during a meeting when a sitter cancelled at the last minute.

Despite the stress, I wouldn't change a thing.

I am a mom who works from home. At first I was apologetic about it and hid the fact as much as possible. Now I'm more open about it. If a client doesn't like the fact that I have a twelve-year-old vice president of operations and a ten-year-old vice president of marketing, then he or she is not the client for me.

Yet working from home with children tests even the most creative women. It's hard to think when the theme song from *Barney and Friends* is playing in the background. (I'm showing my kids' ages by referring to a show that is now most likely passé. I'm ashamed to admit I don't even know what's popular with the younger set these days. Believe it or not, someday you'll be the same way.) It's hard to remain organized when kids insist on messing up your carefully placed "file" piles. And getting out the door for meetings can be difficult with a child wrapped around your leg hollering, "Nooo, Mommy, don't go!"

> Though most work-at-home moms are grateful they can work from home, many express frustration at the juggling required to do so successfully.

I made a huge mistake in my at-home career in thinking I could handle a heavy workload without child care. I was home because I wanted to be the primary caregiver for my children. Regularly arranging for sitters seemed to defeat the purpose of coming home to begin with. So I blithely tried to juggle everything without the necessary support. You've already read what a miserable failure that was in previous chapters.

The majority of moms I surveyed prior to writing this book indicated that finding time to work and not feeling guilty about it challenges them. They feel guilty if their kids want them to play and they have to meet a deadline. It bothers them to hit the Play button on a video in order to find the time to work. Though most are grateful they can work from home, many express frustration at the juggling required to do so successfully.

One woman summed it up this way: "I struggle to find the appropriate mix of balancing my family and mothering responsibilities with my work responsibilities. . . . I wonder every day if I am devoting my time enough in a certain area." Another wrote, "Feels like I'm doing business twenty-four hours a day around my child's schedule."

Here's a critical question all work-at-home moms must face: Does it make more sense to try to "fit business in" around your family's schedule or to have defined work times so that there's clear delineation between your office hours and your home life?

Only you can answer that question for your family and your business. Your answer will be dependent on many things, including:

- number and ages of your children
- type of work you do
- flexibility of your work
- how dependent you are on the income
- individual and family health
- level of spousal and family support
- number and type of other commitments
- availability of child care
- financial resources
- other circumstances unique to your situation

Figuring out the answer to the child care question is like solving a story problem. The more factors there are to consider, the more complicated the process of finding the "right" answer. And what's right for you and your family won't necessarily be right for another woman and her family. That's why, after considering the above influences, you also must *trust your instincts* and *act on what you know*.

Trusting your instincts requires you to develop the ability to listen to what your head and heart tell you internally. Identifying what you're hearing and turning it into action can be difficult since many of us aren't trained to listen to our gut. The process can be nebulous and uncertain, providing even more incentive *not* to trust ourselves. But the more you do it, the easier it becomes.

Most moms have had the experience of suspecting there's something wrong with a child, such as strep throat, allergies, or an ear infection. Though there may be no visible signs, when our instincts scream loudly enough, we pick up the phone and call the doctor. Sometimes the instincts are wrong (and we're relieved) and sometimes they are right on (and we wonder why we don't trust ourselves more).

Your proximity to and experience with your family members heightens your instincts about them. But the more you pay attention to your "gut," the more highly developed your instincts become. One way to handle the child care issue is to ask yourself what your gut is telling you.

Some moms hear their gut telling them their children will benefit from additional socialization, so it's okay for them to use outside child care.

Some moms hear their gut telling them the time isn't right for them to be focusing fully on work, so they choose a work-at-home option that allows them flexibility in how much time they put in each week.

Some moms hear that it's okay to arrange for child care on an as-needed basis.

And some moms hear that the very best thing is for them not to use outside child care and to continue to fit their work in around their family schedule.

Which option is best for you? Trust your instincts. And then act on what you know.

What do you know about your family members and their needs? What do you know about your children's individual personality characteristics? What do you know about your own needs? Smart moms act on what they know.

If you know your child is overwhelmed in large groups, a day care center probably isn't the best choice for you. On the other hand, if you know you're raising a social bug, maybe this is a good option.

When you consider your personal circumstances, act on what you know about your kids, and trust your instincts, you're more likely to develop child care strategies that support your work at home in a way that's comfortable for you and minimizes the "mommy guilt" that seems to be inherent for at-home CEOs.

There's a caveat, however. Just when you think you have everything covered in the home versus work scenario, something may change.

My daughter took daily naps through her entry in kindergarten. My son napped only until the moment I signed the contract to write my first book. The very next day, he gave up napping altogether. No warning. No transition period. He simply was a napper one day and a former napper the next. With the ink on the contract dry and my daughter in preschool three afternoons a week, I had to find an option for my son. A day care had just opened close to our home and hadn't reached capacity. I called the director and asked if she'd consider accepting my son on a very part-time basis. When she said yes, I took a tour, met the teachers, and decided this option would work. It upended my thinking of myself as an "at-home mom" but was necessary because of the commitment I'd made to finish the manuscript.

Three times a week I'd drop my daughter at preschool, then take my son to Pleasant Park. (Why is it that day care names are so similar to retirement home names? I've always wondered.) He arrived a little after 1:00 when all his classmates were napping. So guess what? The child who wouldn't nap at home would lie down quietly on his cot with a book—and quickly fall asleep. Go figure. The irony that I paid the day care to let him nap on their cot when he wouldn't nap in his own bed is not lost on me.

The school year ended, and I took advantage of neighbor girls who were eager to earn a little extra money. They came to my house and played with my children while I worked in my office. When fall arrived, my daughter entered elementary school and my son was able to attend preschool. Three days a week I dropped him off and rushed home and worked for two precious hours. Occasionally he'd have a playdate that would allow me some additional free time. Otherwise, I limited my work and supplemented my office hours with evening and early morning desk visits.

With both kids in school now, my workdays are more predictable. I put the kids on the bus, head to my office, and don't usually come out until 3:20 when the first child bursts through the door after school. I take Tuesdays off for a trip to the gym and the grocery store, and I try to schedule all my personal appointments for this day. For a while I wasn't nearly this disciplined. Not surprisingly, I didn't get as much done. By setting regular office hours for myself, I'm more able to plan wisely and keep up with my workload. It's not as much fun as the previous at-home flexibility I used to enjoy, but I'm a work-at-home mom, and recognizing that helps save my sanity.

Recently I tried a tip I picked up from a woman in one of my work-at-home seminars. She pays her kids $1 a morning to play quietly with each other while she works. Because my children are older, I paid them each $5 to let me work until lunchtime on Martin Luther King's birthday. I went to my office before they woke up and was delighted when my daughter fixed breakfast for herself and my son. (I was even more delighted when she cleaned up after herself in the kitchen!) My office door was open so I could monitor what was going on and knew the kids were safe. They played together for a while and then watched a little T.V. They also showed up at my door promptly at noon for their money, which was okay with me because by then I had conquered my to-do list for the day and was ready to spend time with them.

I suspect there are as many creative ways to handle child care as there are moms working at home. In addition to the above, when my children were young they occasionally spent time with two other at-home moms who provided child care on an "as-needed" basis.

(Thanks, Debbie and Sharon!) I compensated them for their time, which created a win-win situation for all of us. Now we have two grandmothers in town who are wonderful about meeting the kids after school on days I travel and my husband is working. Summer offers a plethora of camps and activities, and I plan my work time accordingly.

Early on in my work-at-home career, I naively believed I could find a "one size fits all" solution to the child care issue. Now I know my solutions have to change as often as the seasons. With a daughter who has completed a babysitting clinic at the local hospital this year and is now old enough to be a sitter herself, we're entering yet another phase of creative child care strategies.

As you ponder the possibilities for your own family, the following tips may be helpful:

Give yourself permission to arrange for child care in addition to your presence at home. Many work-at-home moms have trouble with this simply because they are home precisely so they can be available to their children. Some believe it defeats the purpose if they utilize outside child care resources. But working from home without any child care makes your job as an at-home CEO more difficult. Figure out how much and what type of care you are comfortable with, then stay within the boundaries you've set for yourself. It is possible to be fully at home and effectively utilize additional child care. The two are not mutually exclusive.

> What works for one season in your family's life may not work indefinitely.

Be flexible. What works for one season in your family's life may not work indefinitely. Trust your instincts about what's working and what's not, and pay attention to what your children say about the caregivers you're dependent on. Be responsive to what they reveal, and consider your needs as well as theirs. It's possible to find something that works for everyone, though it may take perseverance to do so.

Be creative. I love the idea of paying my kids to keep themselves busy while I work. (They love it too!) I wouldn't have thought of this on my own, but I'm inspired by the mom who shared the idea with me, and I'm actively looking for other creative possibilities. This idea reminds me to be willing to explore new options as our child care needs continue to evolve.

Have the courage to do what's best for your family. Because you and I are different and our needs and circumstances are not the same, our solution to the child care issue should also be different. That's okay. Too often we look at what other women are doing and adopt the same solutions for ourselves without considering that our values, resources, and experiences are not the same. Your strategy needs to take into account your family's situation and any unique circumstances that influence what's right for you.

Seek support. Because the parental pact is so important, be sure your husband is comfortable with what you are doing. Even if he's not interested in helping you decide what's best or interviewing potential sitters, keep him informed. This keeps things running smoothly and lends itself to family harmony.

If financial resources are tight, trade child care services. Find another mom who works from home with whom you are comfortable exchanging babysitting services and develop an exchange agreement that allows you to regularly watch each other's kids. Make sure you find someone who's reliable so you can count on the regular work time this option provides. While spousal support is important, teaming with other work-at-home moms is valuable, too.

Reevaluate your needs occasionally. As your business evolves, your child care needs will likely change, too. More work may necessitate more child care. A business that's seasonal may require periods of outside child care followed by periods of no assistance at all. As children age, they will be more able to look after themselves, perhaps eliminating your need altogether.

When my children were preschool age, I evaluated my needs on a day-to-day basis. It was stressful to have this issue continually hanging over my head. As I've entered a new season of mothering (the school season!) I'm now able to identify my needs on a monthly basis, which causes far less anxiety. If you're in an early season of mothering, hang on! The child care puzzle gets easier to piece together as your children mature.

Work-at-home moms tell me that child care is one of their most pressing concerns. If it stresses you too, know you are not alone. Give yourself permission to proactively address this issue in a way that works for your family. When you do, you'll be more likely to be a satisfied and effective at-home CEO.

Lesson Learned: Child care may be the toughest issue at-home entrepreneurs wrestle with. Address the issue with energy, creativity, and clear goals, and you're more likely to create a situation that works for every member of your family.

Work-at-Home Mom Profile

Kris Holmin

Name and type of business:

My sister and I own K&K Inspirations, Inc. Our company provides commercial and residential interior consultation, custom window treatments, and blinds.

How long have you been in business?

Five years. My sister and I chose this business because I had always helped friends and family with different projects. Although my degree is in communications, my minor is in graphic design. My sister has an art degree and worked for a design firm before it was purchased by another individual. At that time we decided we should try this on our own.

What's the toughest part of running a business and a family under one roof?

There are many times when it is tough to walk away from it. Often in the evening I am going through fabric samples or doing book work. You don't necessarily leave the work at the office.

What unique child care strategies have you used to enable you to work successfully from home?

When we started the business, my daughter Joanna was eight years old and fairly self-sufficient. One of our major rules is that when I am on the phone, whether it is work related or otherwise, she must find something to entertain herself. Many of my appointments occur on evenings and weekends, and I am fortunate to have the help of my husband when the need arises for someone to stay with Joanna.

What's your favorite part of being in business for yourself?

I can work as hard as I want to, and my schedule is flexible. In the summer I only schedule appointments two days out of the week, and I try to vary those days. If I want to hang with my girl on Friday afternoon by the pool, it is my choice. On a majority of days I pick her up from school. To me that is important because it gives us a chance to go over her day. Flexibility in schedules is huge for me.

What's your least favorite part?

The evening and weekend appointments. Not everyone can meet during the weekdays. Therefore, if you want the business, it takes some sacrifice. But it is tough for me to take family time for appointments.

What do you know now that you wish you would have known when you started?

All of the paperwork involved with running a business. I have the responsibility for all accounting, billing, and ordering. Keeping up with it is a major time commitment.

What's the biggest mistake you've made as an at-home business owner?

We still do not have a promotional plan set in stone for the business. We advertise in the yellow pages, but most of our business comes from referrals and word of mouth. We have continued to grow every year, but our apprehensions include worrying about how much we can handle without sacrificing quality for our clients.

What's the smartest move you've made as an at-home business owner?

We have outstanding customer service. We follow through, we take care of things, basically we do right by the customer, and we consider ourselves to be enjoyable to work with.

What's the most mortifying "mom moment" you've had in running your at-home business?

Early in the business when Joanna was eight or nine, we had a "wine of the month" delivered to our house. I had a client at the house for a meeting, and the gentleman who delivered the wine rang the doorbell. Joanna went to the door, looked out the side window, and yelled, "Mom, the wine guy is here!" At that age she recognized the wine guy—like he was there every day! Lord only knows what my client was thinking. I still giggle when I remember it!

What advice would you give to another woman who is interested in starting her own work-at-home business?

My advice to anyone is "do it!" Why not? If you are organized and have a reputable product or service, definitely at least try. Great rewards are not without great risks.

Learn more about K&K Inspirations, Inc. at www.kkinspirations.com.

8

client crisis—or is it?

One of the stresses of being self-employed is that you are dependent on others for your income. If you're in home-based sales, you rely on hostesses to book you and their guests to buy. If you're in a service business, you count on clients to call, and you pray for the repeat business that will help you build a firm foundation and more regular income. Even those with steady work such as day care or voice lessons experience income fluctuation when people move away or discontinue using their services. The bottom line is that income can be sporadic when you're an entrepreneur. And that can be scary.

The possibility of fluctuating income makes many of us feel beholden to those who pay us. On the surface, it makes sense. To keep my business healthy, I must keep my clients happy. But what about when customers start taking advantage of you? It definitely tests your sanity.

In my book *How to Say No . . . and Live to Tell About It,* I tell the story of a client who took advantage of me—but only because I let him. I'll include it here for the benefit of our discussion:

I learned my lesson, however, when a client took advantage of my willingness to sacrifice family time to meet a deadline. He needed a marketing piece written on short notice. I stayed up late working on the piece and delivered it on time, only to find that he had left for vacation and would be gone for a week. In addition, I learned that he had had the information for the piece for over a month. He just hadn't gotten around to calling me until he was cleaning off his desk so that he could go on vacation.

I was incredulous. I had bought into his crisis, only to discover it really wasn't a crisis. In short, I paid the price for his procrastination.[1]

The above experience was valuable for me as a business owner. I finally have reached the point where I no longer feel compelled to respond to "emergency" projects that have a short turnaround time. It hasn't always been this way. As you know, early on I was afraid to say no for fear I would lose business or alienate potential clients.

However, as I became busier, it became necessary for me to stop saying, "Sure, I can do that!" before checking my calendar and carefully analyzing my workload. Something surprising happened when I became more deliberate about guarding my time. Clients who called and needed a project "yesterday" often actually had time to wait. I remember one who called and needed something within the week. I told him I'd love to work on the project but couldn't start it for two weeks due to my workload. I offered to share the names of a couple other freelancers for his convenience. There was a short silence on the line, and then he said, "I guess it can wait. Would you put us on the schedule?"

It seems crazy, but the busier I got, the more clients seemed willing to wait!

After staying up late (or maybe I should say early since sometimes I went to bed well after midnight) one too many nights and expecting my young children to understand why I was grumpy the next day, I realized that working at home *wasn't* really working.

As I examined my workload and my habits, I recognized I suffered from a classic case of overestimating how much I could do and underestimating how long it would take. It was clear I needed a reality check. You may need one too.

A reality check is simple to conduct. You sit down with your journal or a blank piece of paper, and you answer these questions:

- Do I feel overwhelmed?
- Am I trying to do too much?
- Are my work commitments forcing me to make sacrifices that are hurting my role as a mom?
- Am I often overly optimistic about how much I can accomplish in a day or week?
- Do those around me seem stressed or out of sorts because of my workload?
- What would happen if I tried to space out my work more evenly?
- Would I lose business if I were more realistic about my deadlines? And if so, would it matter?
- Am I working at a pace I can sustain over the long haul? If not, how can I get to that point?

I know that if you're running a direct sales or network marketing business, often you have initial goals your company requires you to meet (i.e., number of parties booked within a month, minimum sales revenue, etc.). This is designed to help get you off to a strong start and to create the momentum necessary to establish you strongly in the business. Even if you're not running a network marketing business, the beginning stages of an enterprise often require more work than do the following phases. This is natural and to be expected. But once you're up and running, you should consider how well the pace of your business works with the pace of your family.

I personally found it difficult to respond to client requests for short turnaround assignments, especially if it required conducting interviews by phone. Many times I was called at the last minute to handle a project that internal staff couldn't complete. Though I'd make all my outbound calls during nap time, it was rare that someone I wanted to interview would return the call while my children slumbered peacefully. More often they'd call at the end of the workday during the "witching hour" when I was doing everything I could to keep my children from melting down while I tried to prepare dinner. Talk about stress!

> Consider how well the pace of your business works with the pace of your family.

Eventually it became clear that writing short pieces wasn't working with my season of at-home mothering. I resigned as a contributing writer for a medical journal and focused instead on speaking, which took me away from home to deliver my work product. That solved the witching hour stress. In addition, it gave me the space to consider writing longer pieces. Instead of writing for others, I began writing things I was more interested in.

My personal reality check is what led me into writing books since short projects weren't working for me. Though they take longer to complete, I now set my own schedule and control the workload. And with my kids in school, it's perfect for this season of at-home mothering.

Are you guilty of letting customer crises add to your stress? Maybe a hostess is late getting her party invitations out, so instead of suggesting an alternative date, you stick with the original one but have a less-than-stellar turnout and disappointing sales. Or maybe you continue to pursue a wayward order long after you should simply because you feel obligated to the individual who says she wants to place it, even though her actions say otherwise.

If you're in a service business such as graphic design or freelance writing, is your schedule full of steady work or "rush" jobs? Be honest. It's difficult to create a sustainable business on the latter.

If you tutor or teach lessons of some sort, do you have customers who don't pay regularly, causing their money crisis to become yours? If so, here's a valuable truth: *you get the behavior you expect.*

When you're clear about your own expectations, it's easier for your customers and clients to meet them. If you haven't taken the time to determine your expectations, it's impossible for you to convey them to the people you work with.

When you refuse to buy into a client crisis, clients will choose not to bring them to you. And if they don't bring them to you, you won't have the difficult task of telling them no.

The following ideas will help minimize the number of client crises you have to respond to in order to help you build a steady and sustainable business:

Decide that you won't be a rescuer. Many women have told me they like to be the one to save the day. That's okay as long as it doesn't compromise your commitment to your family. Under what circumstances will you choose to help a client? Think about it before you're faced with the situation, and you're more likely to respond in a way that's comfortable for both of you.

Don't hesitate to negotiate. This is a powerful but underutilized option for business owners. If you can't meet a customer request, offer an alternative. Here's how it works. Simply say, "Though I'm not able to book a party on Monday of that week, I could do it Tuesday, Wednesday, or the following Monday. Which is best for you?" Or, "I can't accept any additional work at this time, but if you're able to wait a week, I'd be happy to help."

Many at-home business owners have been surprised to learn that suggesting an alternative doesn't necessarily mean lost business. In fact, customers are impressed when they know you're in demand. It reminds me of a piece of advice I once heard: if you want to be successful, appear busy.

Develop policies. If you've read any of my previous books, you know I'm a big fan of policies simply because they make managing easier. I have payment policies, booking policies, reimbursement policies, and workload policies. Because I limit the number of overnight speaking engagements I accept, I can more easily handle scheduling decisions. Since I know that my workload is traditionally heavy in the spring, my policy is not to volunteer for time-intensive projects from February through April.

In addition to making management easier, policies help ensure effectiveness. I choose not to accept speaking engagements less than two weeks prior to the date of the event simply because it doesn't allow me enough preparation time.

What policies would help you manage your business more effectively? Maybe you'll develop a policy for the maximum number of demonstrations you'll book in a week. This will allow you to meet your commitment to your family, guard your sanity, and be responsive to the parental pact you have with your husband. Maybe you'll choose to require a lead time of at least three weeks prior to booking an event so that the hostess has sufficient time to get invitations in the mail. Maybe you'll require payment for your tutoring services in advance, due by the first of the month.

Not only do policies help you manage your business more effectively, they also help you convey your expectations to your customers and clients. And remember, you get the behavior you expect.

Consider charging rush fees. It's standard procedure for some freelancers to charge time-and-a-half for work they do that requires a short turnaround. One at-home mom I know started doing this to discourage clients from calling at the last minute. Later she confessed she actually likes these types of projects because she gets paid more for doing the same amount of work! She jokingly refers to herself as a "rush junkie." By charging a rush fee, she ensures there will be a bottom-line benefit for her family when she works on last-minute projects. Consider creating this type of policy if it would work for your business.

Another mom who responded to my online survey wrote, "An ad agency would charge a rush time fee if they were expected to turn a project around in a couple of days, but since I work at home without regular hours, I'm expected to do it at my regular rate."

Hold on there, mama! *You get the behavior you expect.* In fact, you're the one responsible for training your clients how to treat you. I know it sounds odd, but let me share a story.

I worked with a freelancer who, though she had a variety of clients, was dependent on one who provided most of her work. This client was moody, demanding, sometimes rude, and often angry. The client's poor behavior stressed out the freelancer, but she felt helpless to make a change until she recognized the physical and mental toll of the relationship.

I encouraged her to identify what she didn't like about the client and to identify ways she might be able to "retrain" the client. When the client yelled on the phone, the freelancer would say, "I can tell you're upset. Perhaps we should talk about this again later." When she made demands for a quick turnaround, the freelancer would say, "I have that scheduled for Thursday of this week. We'll get it to you by Friday at the latest." When the client asked, "Don't you like working for me?" the freelancer would say, "This isn't a matter of like or dislike; it's a matter of scheduling." In addition, the freelancer set new turnaround policies for all of her clients, including the difficult one.

As of this writing, the "retraining" is going well. There have been some tense times, but the freelancer says she feels "so much better," and she's empowered by the fact that she stood up for herself and started acting like an at-home CEO.

You get the behavior you expect. You might think a client expects you to do a rush job at no additional charge because you "work from home." But the reality may be that you're grateful for the work, afraid of losing it, and consequently will do anything to keep it. I'd

You get the behavior you expect.

be willing to bet that if you start charging a rush fee, you'll quickly find the requests for a quick turnaround decreasing. And if they don't, you'll have more income to show for the inconvenience and stress.

Develop a referral network. I have several colleagues I often refer business to when I can't accept it myself. It makes it easier for me to turn down work because I know my client will receive the help he or she needs without me.

I make two types of referrals. First, I make a referral if I'm already booked or my schedule is too tight. Second, I refer business when a potential client can't afford my fees. It took me a long time to reach the point where I was comfortable passing business along, but I've since learned this is a great way to provide for a client's needs while allowing myself to grow to the next level of business. Now I actively seek mentoring opportunities and willingly pass my protégés' names along to clients. This creates a win-win situation for everyone.

Are you a crisis junkie? Some of us are. It makes us feel needed and wanted (a feeling we don't always get from home). You can determine your junkie status by analyzing how you feel when you help "save" someone or something. In addition, if you catch yourself saying or thinking the words, "I *have* to" or "I *must*," you may well have the savior complex. There truly is no "have to" or "must." Everything in life is a choice. I've trained myself so that when I hear myself use those words, I think twice about the situation. This may be a valuable exercise for you as well.

Lesson Learned: Stress comes from saving clients and customers. Sanity is compromised when we routinely buy into others' crises. Decide you'll help when you can, but realize that the world won't stop spinning when you choose to say no.

9

systematizing your business for maximum effectiveness

If you want to create calm out of chaos, you'll take this advice that I know to be essential to success: systematize whatever you can in your business.

If you're a representative in a network marketing business, you're lucky. This has already been done for you. When you began, a mentor (or "upline") took you under his or her wing and showed you the ropes. How to book parties or demonstrations. How to take orders. How to place orders. How often to call for reorders. You may have even learned some secrets to help increase your sales or bookings, including phrases designed to make you more successful.

At one direct sales event where I spoke, I heard a regional manager say, "If you do exactly what I tell you, I guarantee you'll be successful." She had done exactly what her manager had told her to do, and it worked. That's how she could guarantee the same success for her team. Her company had a system, and by teaching this system to newcomers, the company was wildly successful. It's this same concept that makes franchises more likely to succeed. Overall, franchises have a success rate of 95 percent in contrast to the 50-plus percent failure rate of new independently owned businesses. Though 80 percent of all businesses fail in the first five years, 75 percent of franchises succeed.

Why? It's the system.

If you're in a network marketing company, when you were learning the business, you likely learned how much profit you'd make on an average event. You probably know the amount of an average sale, how many people who RSVP actually show up, and what percentage of attendees will book an event of their own. For many entrepreneurs it takes months, if not years, to learn this information. Since you know it already, you're ahead of the game.

But what if you're not working as a consultant for a large company?

> Systematizing your business will free you from fretting over the details and give you the time and energy to think about how to take your business to the next level.

Systematize everything you can. Doing so will free you from fretting over the details and give you the time and energy to think about how to take your business to the next level.

I resisted this step for years and now regret it. When I think back to the stress that ensued as a result, I could just kick myself.

So how do you systematize your business? Easy. Walk through an encounter with a client from beginning to end and automate the process.

Let's say Polly Pianist teaches piano lessons from home two nights a week. She's been in business for a year now, and though she has limited slots available for students, there is some turnover due to kids losing interest, finding jobs, or leaving for college and families moving out of the area, among other things. Currently she has two openings, which obviously reduces her income.

Over the past year Polly has fielded several phone calls from parents looking for a piano instructor. But she doesn't have a system in place for capturing these names on a waiting list. Instead she writes names down on Post-it notes which inevitably get stuck to other pieces of paper and eventually are lost. In fact, Polly knows she has at least three families interested in taking lessons from her—she just can't find where she's written their names. Polly needs a system.

In less than ten minutes Polly could organize this aspect of her business. She simply needs to write the words "Waiting List" on the outside of a file folder and put the file folder where she knows she can find it. When a parent calls to inquire about lessons, Polly grabs the folder and records the individual's name, phone number, mailing address, and email address on a sheet kept in the folder for this purpose. Then she takes out a form letter stored in the folder, addresses it, and sends it to the parent. The form letter includes her expectations and her studio policies. With a little thought, Polly can "automate" this aspect of her business.

Not only would systematizing help save Polly time and frustration since she no longer has to search in vain for lost sticky notes, it also would help her communicate efficiently with potential students. Instead of verbally covering her expectations, she simply mails them. Then, when a slot opens up and a student is accepted into the studio, she could ask both the student and his or her parent to sign the document. Thus policies are spelled out in writing, helping to ensure understanding and teamwork between Polly, her students, and their parents.

What can you automate in your business? Perhaps you need to develop a database designed to let you know when it's time to call customers for reorders. Or maybe you need to develop a contact form like Polly's. Or perhaps you need a mailing system designed to communicate with prospects so they'll have your information when it's time to get in touch with you.

Though I'm telling you to systematize your business, I stupidly spent the first years of mine reinventing the wheel every time a potential client called. Instead of having a form, I'd reach for a pad of paper and start taking notes. Inevitably, after a call I'd realize I had failed to capture a valuable piece of information, such as where an event was going to be held, how long it would last, or how many people would be in the audience. To follow up with each prospect, I'd have to call or email a request for the missing information before I could provide fee information. Not only did this require more of my time, it made me look less than professional.

Even though I knew I would benefit from having event forms, client questionnaires, and sample rate charts available early on in my business, I kept telling myself I was too busy to create them. That was lame-brained thinking!

Now if you call my office, the first thing I do is grab a form. I start by recording your name and contact information and what you're calling about, and then I ask a series of questions designed to make it easy for me to follow up after our call. I also grab a file folder and write your organization's name on the outside—something else I resisted for years, though I have no idea why. Maybe it was because I was working part-time and didn't think I needed the organization required by a full-timer. How silly of me. The form is the first piece of paper to go into the file and will remain there as long as I have the file. In addition to including all the details of the engagement, I also record the date when I send follow-up information, including a thank-you note after the event. Remember, the goal is to automate everything.

See how this streamlines my interaction with clients and frees me to begin thinking about how I can better serve them rather than focusing on the details?

Recently I've been coaching a graphic designer on a variety of aspects of her business. One of her goals is to work less and make more money. Consequently, we're looking at how she can turn one-time clients into long-term customers so that she doesn't have to focus regularly on new business development. Within two weeks of our first consultation, she forwarded two emails to me. Both were from prospective clients looking to develop a long-term relationship with someone who could help meet their marketing needs.

Because she didn't have a client questionnaire, that was one of the first tasks she tackled. Now when a client calls, she can either use the document as a guideline and record the answers herself or, if it's appropriate, she can ask the client to complete the document at his or her convenience and return it to her. This helps ensure she has good background information before making a recommendation. When she receives a request for a proposal, she can use this internal document to determine what else, if anything, she needs to know before responding.

The second task she addressed was creating a proposal for a client. Now she has a structured document that includes information about her training and background, a partial client list, and samples of her work. The next time she's asked for a proposal, she'll simply customize this template, something that will save her time while professionally marketing her business.

What can you automate and systematize for your business? Start by answering these questions:

- What do you do repeatedly that could be simplified with a form or a system?
- What do you like least about your business, and is there a way to reduce the time you spend on this task by streamlining the process?
- What details ensure success for your business, and how can you more effectively capture, record, and store them? (Consider using databases, specially developed forms, etc.)
- What would require less brainpower if you could create a system to deal with it?
- What goes wrong most often in your business, and what kind of system would reduce the chance of error?

These are just a few questions designed to prompt your thinking about what you can automate and systematize. Doing so frees you to think about how to take your business to the next level rather than struggling just to survive. It's a terrifically simple concept, I know, so why don't more entrepreneurs use it? Mostly because we're so busy juggling home and business that we don't think we have the time to take a step back to see what systems would help us be more efficient. Though it *takes* time in the short run, systematizing *saves* time in the long run.

> Though it *takes* time in the short run, systematizing *saves* time in the long run.

There's another benefit as well. As your business grows, having a system makes it easier to teach others how to help you. If I wanted to, I could more easily hire an assistant now that I've systematized my business. The event form would make it easy for someone else to field calls, capture necessary information, and tell callers that I'll be in touch within twenty-four hours. Information about my business appears on paper rather than being stored in my head. I've taken what's routine and made it even more so, thereby enabling me to focus more fully on serving clients in the best way possible. Since I no longer have to use brainpower to handle the initial contact and event details, I can focus instead on innovation, further developing myself and my skills, and planning for the future. As I do that, I increase the chances that I'll be able to increase my revenue in the years to come.

Lesson Learned: Systems support effective and profitable businesses and make them even more successful.

Work-at-Home Mom Profile

Lisa Weitzel

Name and type of business:
Lisa Weitzel Photography. I'm a freelance photographer.

How long have you been in business?
I'm beginning my fourth official year in business.

Why did you choose this business?
It chose me, actually. I took lots of photos as a hobby. After people saw my photos, they began to offer me money to photograph them.

What's the toughest part of running a business and a family under one roof?
When you own your own business and run it from home, you are always at work. Clients call me at all hours, and it's hard to draw boundary lines. The hardest part is defining those lines and not taking a call or answering an email because I believe in putting my family first.

What unique child care strategies have you used to enable you to work successfully from home?
I have been lucky enough that my oldest child has been able to watch her younger brother. Most of my jobs are after normal business hours, so my husband is able to help as well.

What's your favorite part of being in business for yourself?
Working in my pj's! Actually, the flexibility is my favorite part. I am still able to volunteer at school or take two weeks off for vacation in the summer when I want to.

What's your least favorite part?
Not having anyone to help or to bounce ideas off of. Sometimes I just get lonely.

What do you know now that you wish you would have known when you started?
Too many things to list!

What's the biggest mistake you've made as an at-home business owner?

Not evaluating my expenses correctly and therefore not charging my clients enough.

What's the smartest move you've made as an at-home business owner?

Using an accountant!

What's the most mortifying "mom moment" you've had in running your at-home business?

My sister called with a crisis right before new clients arrived. They walked in, and I apologized and handed the phone to my daughter to work it out with my sister. Nothing like forcing my fifteen-year-old to grow up quickly!

What advice would you give to another woman who is interested in starting her own work-at-home business?

Have some sort of schedule to your days. I still don't, and it's hard to compartmentalize my professional work and my home work. I also make the mistake of not charging my friends for my services. If I went to their place of business, I would have to pay, but that's a very difficult battle for me to win.

Learn more about Lisa Weitzel Photography at www.lisaweitzel.com.

10

refreshment

learning the art of taking a break

Why is it that when a child wakes up in the middle of the night and needs reassurance, he goes to mom's side of the bed? Why is it that mom often has a child on her lap when she's sitting on the toilet? And why is it that when a child needs to throw up, he chooses to do it on mom instead of dad?

These are mysteries that will remain unsolved in our lifetime. Yet they are the very mysteries that make mothering such an incredibly profound experience—and working at home such an intense one. To divide oneself between children and adults, between Play-Doh and QuickBooks, and between email and the Disney Channel requires shape-shifting abilities that mere mortals often don't possess. Somehow, we as work-at-home moms must develop the skill.

But the skill comes with a price. Moving from one world to the next, from one mind-set to another, and from caretaker to decision maker repeatedly throughout the course of a day is physically and mentally exhausting in a way others can't understand unless they've done it. As David Goetz writes, "it's not only the actual work; it's the space it occupies in your mind; like rain in the desert, thoughts of survival and success seep into every crack and soak deep into the subconscious."[1]

Heroics like ours deserve a time of renewal and refreshment. It may be time we have to beg and fight for, or it may be time we can build into our schedule each week, depending on our circumstances. Regardless, it's time that pays dividends—both for our business and our very souls.

What refreshes you? Some long for solitude, while others crave interaction with other adults. For some of us, a latte with a friend will energize us for a month, while others prefer a quiet stroll down a bookstore shelf line. Some crave an extra hour of sleep, while others thrive on an early morning run. It doesn't really matter what it is that refreshes you. What matters is that you are clever enough to find a way to work it into your schedule.

"Doesn't everyone need refreshment?" you might ask. The obvious answer is yes.

"Don't all working moms need renewal?" you might query. The obvious answer to that is also yes.

But living and working under one roof can lead to a restlessness that's hard to fathom, difficult to explain, and sometimes even harder for us to recognize in ourselves. I've been antsy before without being able to identify where the wanderlust is coming from or even recognize it for what it is. Eventually I was able to connect the dots and recognize that the challenge of being available and present for both clients and my family simultaneously is the very thing that makes refreshment so important to me. Here's how you can take advantage of regular refreshment as well:

> The challenge of being available and present for both clients and family simultaneously is the very thing that makes refreshment so important.

Get out regularly. Even when I'm on deadline for a project, I make sure I get out of the house, if only to take a walk around the block or run to the grocery store for milk. Doing so forces me to interact with more than just the family pets and keeps me from turning into a recluse.

When my kids were young, I found sanity at the library, where we all could read quietly, or at the park, where they could run and jump while I made a to-do list.

Schedule it. I routinely sit down with my calendar on Sunday night and determine where in my schedule I can find time for refreshment. I go to the gym regularly, participate in a Bible study, attend a Moms' Night Out several times a year, meet with two writer friends occasionally, cook with a group of women every other month, and make sure I schedule thinking time in which I can sit and stare at the walls if that's what I need. I also used to trade babysitting with a friend to find the solitude I needed to feed my soul.

Be creative. Turn your bathroom into a retreat with candles and soft music. Wait until the kids are in bed or ask your husband to help keep them away from the locked door—which has a magnetic pull for children for some unknown reason. Lunch on a healthy salad from McDonald's while you watch your children in the Playland on the other side of the Plexiglas. (You can see them, but you can't hear them!) Play library at home and let your children check out a book to read while you do the same. Teach your children that quiet time is healthy, just like food and sleep, and therefore should be welcomed instead of despised. Put yourself in "time out" while your kids watch you take a break (and remember that you get one minute for every year of your age!).

Recognize your specific needs. They say a man's home is his castle, and that's certainly true for my husband, Stuart. For years he left his castle for the office five days a week, and by Friday he was ready to return and put his feet up. On the other hand, sometimes I don't leave home for days, and by Friday I'm itching to get out. Even the best marriages can be challenged by the conflicting need to stay in versus go out. To keep this from being an area of conflict for us, I've learned to give Stuart an early heads up if I'm stir crazy, and he's learned that sometimes it benefits all of us if I get out of the house.

Have a standing date. A couple who took me under their wing my first year of college had a standing lunch date on Mondays. They used that time to discuss the events of the weekend, to discuss what was ahead for the week, and to make plans for the coming weekend.

You can adapt this idea for yourself, whether it's lunching with your spouse or a friend, meeting someone for a walk through the park, getting your nails done, or meeting with a different client or prospect each week to promote your business. Several times a year I ask myself who I'd like to get to know better. Then I pick up the phone and invite them to lunch. (If the resulting conversation is work-related, I keep the receipt and write off the expense.) Not only has this helped refuel me, it's helped me develop a valuable network over the years.

To make this time away from the office as effective as possible, consider running errands on the way to and from your final destination. That way you'll be able to focus solely on work when you return to your home office.

Build a work-at-home network. I have several friends who work from home. Occasionally I'll call and connect with another at-home entrepreneur when I'm feeling restless or isolated. It's helpful knowing other women experience what I do. It's also helpful to have a network I can call on when I'm stuck with a business dilemma—and I'm happy to reciprocate when these friends need advice as well. Navigating the challenges of working from home is less lonely when you know other moms are walking in your shoes.

Take your work off-site. For years I've heard other writers talk about how much work they get done at their local coffee shop. Though I prefer to write in solitude and silence, two weeks ago I decided to give this a try. I packed up my laptop, treated myself to breakfast, and then settled down to write next to the fireplace at a local restaurant. It took a while for me to be able to drown out others' conversations, but once I did, I managed to get a good deal of work done. And I was fireside in a comfy chair!

When the weather is nice, I personally am partial to writing outside. I'll either take my laptop to a shaded area in our backyard or drive to a park and sit on a bench.

Your work may or may not be mobile. If it is, consider changing your scenery to help defeat any isolation you may feel as a solopreneur. Many women I interviewed said that getting away from home helps save their sanity.

Participate in group exercise. I started attending a body sculpting class with a friend on Tuesday mornings last year. The class is an hour and a half long, and I barely made it through the first time I attended. While others were lifting eight- and ten-pound weights, I was lifting three-pounders. When others did twenty-five push-ups, I was lucky to hit ten. I was so sore I could hardly get out of bed the next day.

Since then I've upped my weights, and though I don't like push-ups any more than I did last year, at least I can keep up. I enjoy the camaraderie with the other women in the class and now plan my Tuesdays around my attendance. In addition to addressing the issue of refueling, this obviously has physical health benefits for me as well.

Volunteer—but don't overdo it. Many moms identified flexibility as one of their favorite aspects of working from home. They like being able to volunteer for school field trips or in their children's classrooms. They enjoy participating in their church, and they thrive on being involved in the community. These worthy activities are valuable ways to contribute to your refreshment as long as your volunteer work doesn't overtake your for-profit work and challenge your ability to keep things in balance at home.

At one point in my work-at-home career, I had to resign all of my volunteer activities to regain balance. Then I slowly began to add things back into my schedule. I'm still careful to remind myself that I work at home and because of that, I can't volunteer for everything I'd like.

Give yourself some time off. When you work for yourself, you don't get any paid vacation or paid sick days, but be sure to take them anyway! I find I am more productive if I periodically take a day off to focus on responsibilities other than work.

Establish quiet time each day. Pick a time of day that works best for you. Most moms I know choose midmorning or midafternoon to coincide with any nap times that still occur. Let your children know that quiet time will occur each day and how long it will last. Establish your expectations up front. When we still had quiet time, the rules were simple: everyone had to be in their own room (mommy's "room" was her office) and on their bed. They could read or play quietly. My purpose for requiring them to be on their bed was that a child who said he or she wasn't sleepy would sometimes fall asleep, giving them needed rest and me needed quiet. Children were allowed to leave their room during this time only for a trip to the bathroom.

Negotiate evening office time to lower your stress. I know two moms who have evening office hours, both with the full support of their husbands. After the dinner dishes are cleared, these women retreat to their office while dad takes over as homework proctor and shower scheduler. These women come out in time for bedtime prayers and tuck-ins, then return to complete their work for the evening. One told me that sometimes knowing she has Thursday evenings free for work is the only thing that keeps her sane as she struggles to balance work with the needs of her preschool-age children while her husband is away during the day.

It's amazing how just a few dedicated minutes can help refresh a weary soul. The longer you ignore your thirst, however, the more you'll have to drink to reverse the dehydration of your spirit. Don't let it happen to you. Instead, drink before you need it.

Lesson Learned: It's better to plan for regular refreshment and renewal than it is to respond to an emergency brought on by burnout and fatigue.

11

facing the daily dinner dilemma

Food. You can't live without it. But plenty of work-at-home moms told me it's a source of stress for them, and they asked me to provide suggestions and ideas for how to beat the dinnertime blues.

No problem. Except that I suffer from them also. And after this week's menu of frozen pizza and chicken strips, I think my family is suffering from them too.

Like many work-at-home moms, I've been flummoxed by why getting dinner on the table is such an ongoing challenge. But after a week under a heavy workload, I finally figured it out. As a solopreneur, I do it all. I'm the president, janitor, human resources director, and technology support staff. My day rarely has a neat beginning or ending, and often I'm still wrapping up my work when I should be starting dinner.

Since the dinner dilemma also challenges me, I would be hypocritical to tackle the topic on my own. So I turned to two professional Supper Queens and asked for their advice. Trish Berg, author of *The Great American Supper Swap*, and Mary Beth Lagerborg, coauthor of *Once-a-Month Cooking*, were both kind enough to contribute to this chapter. Thanks to them, we all can restore sanity to both the kitchen and the dinner hour. Take it away, girls!

Become a Supper Swap Mom
By Trish Berg

Every afternoon that "what's for dinner" question can creep into your life and easily steal your joy. Motherhood is busy, especially if you are working from home, and moms need a simpler way to do dinner. That's where supper swapping comes in. Imagine, if you will, *Extreme Makeover: Home Edition* meets *Wife Swap*.

Not really. But close. Supper swapping does make over a busy family's life in an extreme way, but you swap suppers, not wives. (Whew!)

Busy families coast to coast are swapping suppers and eliminating that "it's 4:30 and nothing's in the oven" panic, and here's why:

- Women today still do 80 percent of the cooking in the home.
- Supper swapping cuts a busy mom's cooking by 50 to 80 percent.
- Supper swapping can save families $4,000 a year or more.
- Only 50 percent of American families are eating supper together on a regular basis.
- Of those meals, 34 percent are coming from fast food and takeout.
- Children who eat supper with their families five to seven times a week are 59 percent less likely to smoke cigarettes, 57 percent less likely to drink alcohol, and 66 percent less likely to try marijuana as teenagers.

So what is supper swapping? Moms helping moms. You prepare one main dish in bulk (times three or four) one day a week, keep one meal for your family, and deliver the rest to the families in your swapping group. The rest of the week someone delivers supper to you!

Supper swapping maximizes your labor. It is much simpler to shop for the ingredients for and then prepare three to five identical meals than it is to shop for and prepare completely different meals. For one to two hours of meal preparation and less than thirty minutes of meal delivery time one day a week, you have an entire week's worth of homemade meals for your family to enjoy.

Supper swapping groups can take many forms, from friends and neighbors to co-workers or extended family members. Any form of community has the potential to be a successful supper swapping group.

You can start small, with just one friend. If there are two of you swapping, you would triple a meal one day a week, deliver one to your friend, freeze one, and eat one. Then she can do the same another day that week. With leftovers, you have at least two to three meals taken care of. And as the weeks go on, you will also have other meals in your freezer you can pull out on non-swapping nights.

My current group consists of four moms, and we swap daily. My typical supper swapping week looks like this:

Monday: Nann delivers pork chops and mashed potatoes at 5:30 p.m., hot and ready to eat.

Tuesday: Kelly delivers pasta ham bake and tossed salad at noon, prepared but not yet cooked, with cooking instructions taped to the lid.

Wednesday: Nancy delivers cheeseburger soup and bread sticks at 1:00 p.m. That night after supper, I prepare four meals of crispy baked chicken and wild rice and put them in our fridge.

Thursday: I drive Riley to preschool at noon, and on the way home I deliver the crispy baked chicken to Nann, Kelly, and Nancy.

Friday: We usually eat leftovers from the week's supper swapping meals, or I make something simple like sandwiches or pancakes.

Supper swapping is flexible and can be tailored to meet the needs of the families involved. We swap daily, but some groups swap weekly or even monthly, combining freezer cooking with supper swapping.

To get started, do a family S.W.A.P. Analysis:

Satisfaction—How satisfied are you with your current family suppers?

Willingness—Are you willing to try supper swapping?

Advantages—How would your family benefit from supper swapping?

Possibilities—Who could you ask to join your group?

Are you ready for an extreme supper makeover? If so, get swapping!

What to Bring to Your First Meeting

- Day planners—to decide on cooking days and delivery times
- Recipe cards or books—to choose three months' worth of meals you will prepare (typically 12–15 recipes per person)
- Blank meal calendars—to fill in with all the details decided upon at the meeting (see www.TrishBerg.com for printable calendars)

What to Decide at Your First Meeting

- Swapping schedule—will you swap daily, weekly, or monthly?

- Time frame—how many months of meals will you plan at a time? (We plan 3 months at a time.)
- Delivery days and times—who will deliver supper on what days, at what times?
- Meal size—will you swap a main dish only, or a main and a side? What portion size? (We use 9 x 13 Pyrex pans with blue lids.)
- Food challenges—how will you handle food allergies or dislikes?
- Delivery—does someone need to be home when you deliver your meals? (You can exchange house keys or garage door codes or leave a cooler with ice in it on the front porch if you can't be home.)
- Meal evaluation—how will the group evaluate the meals? Honesty and flexibility are key here.
- Pans—how will you handle rotating pans through the group?
- Last-minute changes—how will you handle last-minute meal changes or cancellations?
- Swapping life cycle—how much notice is needed when someone wants to leave the group? (We ask for one month's notice.)

Once-a-Month Cooking

By Mary Beth Lagerborg

The proximity of the kitchen to the at-home office leaves us more vulnerable to the daily looming stress of what's for dinner. Surely if we are working from home, we can get a meal on the table. Right?

Right—if we do some menu planning so that the process doesn't eat us and our precious work time alive with worrying about what to make, running to the store, preparing it, and cleaning it up.

"Once-a-month cooking" is a meal-planning method devised by me and my friend Mimi Wilson. Our book by the same name takes you step-by-step through the process of preparing a month's dinner entrées at a time and freezing them. The book also includes two-week menu cycles for the first-timer getting used to the method or for the smaller family that could easily eat off these entrées, packaged in smaller portions, for nearly a month.

The secret of the method is that you do all similar processes at once: cook all the chicken, brown all the ground beef, chop all the vegetables. You shop one day or evening, then the next day or evening you cook—making one big mess and then minimizing it on succeeding evenings.

If you have tried this, you know that gazing into a well-stocked freezer housing a wide variety of tasty entrées at the ready is a near-spiritual experience. It's that utter preparedness that is so appealing. The method is also economical because you can shop for food in bulk and remove the need to continually fall back on the more expensive options of Chinese takeout, pizza delivery, or eating out.

In comparison with meal preparation franchises such as Dream Dinners or Supper Solutions, you have your choice of menus and can customize by preparing and packaging portions to fit your family size (or perhaps your family plus a portion divided off for elderly parents). And you have some larger entrées on-the-ready for having company. When a family member is on a special diet, once-a-month cooking addresses the need for the rest of the family to eat well without your constantly thinking up two menus.

> Once-a-month cooking helps you maximize your work time and minimize your time in the kitchen.

Once-a-month cooking doesn't require a big chest freezer (many entrées are frozen in bags), nor do you need to be well-organized or a good cook (the book takes you by the hand to get it done). And family members can easily help with the final cooking and prepara-

Author's Note: Trish and Mary Beth have graciously shared some of their favorite recipes for your benefit. To solve your dinner dilemma, turn to the appendix on page 204 for their recipes and get cooking! I hope the recipes will whet your appetite for their books, which are available in bookstores or online. For more valuable resources or to buy these books, I urge you to visit www.TrishBerg.com and www.dwellingspace.com.

tion of a vegetable, salad, and bread near serving time (and help with the monthly big cooking day, for that matter!).

Our motive in developing the method was to provide a way to get nutritious meals to the table conveniently so that good interaction can happen there. As a result, *Once-a-Month Cooking* includes many Table Talk questions to get solid, out-of-the-rut conversation flowing. Another benefit is that it's easy to have company more often, with an entrée already on hand!

You simply plan ahead. Prepare. Freeze. Thaw. Eat! Once-a-month cooking solves the "What's for dinner?" dilemma in a way that makes it possible for you to maximize your work time and minimize your time in the kitchen, making it easier for work-at-home to work.

Swap, Freeze, or Both?

Based on what I learned from Trish and Mary Beth, recently some friends and I combined the idea of freezer cooking with supper swapping and had a great evening in the process. Stuart and I met with three other couples. Each was assigned a recipe prior to the event and was responsible for bringing enough ingredients to prepare four family-size servings of their respective dish. One by one we prepared each recipe. Whoever brought the ingredients was responsible for walking the rest of the group through the process. At the end of the evening, each couple had four meals to take home with them—kind of like an adult treat bag similar to those given out at kids' birthday parties, except our treat bags each fed our family a delicious, home-cooked meal!

Not only did the evening serve the greater purpose of feeding our families, but it also fed our spirits as we laughed and enjoyed each others' company while we worked. We had so much fun, we did it again shortly thereafter. I assigned meals, another couple hosted, yet another brought appetizers, and the fourth provided a delicious dessert. Our hostess provided prizes for silly cooking categories such as funniest, neatest, and grouchiest chef.

I suspect we'll do it again, though I don't know when. One couple found the make-ahead aspect so wonderful that they recently prepared and froze eleven meals for their family!

Though I've only used make-ahead cooking on a limited basis, my favorite aspect of it is that it's comforting to know I have treasure in my freezer. When scheduling gets tight or I know I'm going to have a full day, it's a treat to be able to grab a meal, defrost it, and know that I have one less thing to worry about. Based on Trish's suggestions, I'm going to look into supper swapping as well.

My busy periods are the times I think I'm most unable to use the tips in this chapter. But I can see that a tight schedule is the perfect time to use a little preplanning to eliminate the dinner dilemma.

> A tight schedule is the perfect time to use a little preplanning in order to eliminate the dinner dilemma.

And, of course, there's always Plan B. These are the nights I close the kitchen and head out with the family for dinner. I use this plan sparingly. Sometimes just knowing I could go out if I really wanted to is enough to motivate me to open the refrigerator and see what I can come up with. On the nights I don't find anything worthwhile, there are always pancakes or scrambled eggs. Eating breakfast for your evening meal is a surefire way to solve the dinner dilemma, and your kids will love it!

Lesson Learned: A little planning ahead eliminates experiencing a daily dilemma and restores sanity to your dinner hour.

Work-at-Home Mom Profile

Sue Schwartz

Name and type of business:

Two businesses: Imagine Designs and Studio on 6th.

How long have you been in business?

Imagine Designs has been in existence for six years and Studio on 6th for four years.

Why did you choose this business?

Imagine Designs grew out of my passion for painting and creating colorful items for the home. Studio on 6th (a consortium of artists) was a result of my painting business. If I had to get my work out there for all to see, I knew that others would have the same hurdle to jump. When we moved our daughter to college in Arizona, we came upon an artful town with an artists' co-op, and the seed was planted.

What's the toughest part of running a business and family under one roof?

The balance of time and space. I work around the schedules of my family and do not have a "place" to paint other than on my kitchen island, which means I have to set up and put away all my work every day.

What unique child care strategies have you used to enable you to work successfully from home?

My children are grown, so this is not a struggle I encounter.

What's your favorite part of being in business for yourself?

My success and my failures are a direct result of my work ethic. I believe that what you put into a business, you get out of the business. I also like the flexibility it affords me. My children are both living in the West, which means much travel, and being my own boss allows me to be able to get my "child" fix in often.

What's your least favorite part?

Probably owning the Studio on 6th. I have responsibility for sixty-plus artists and all the decisions and refereeing that needs to be done with that many "artistic" people.

I have all the decisions on my shoulders, and sometimes it is overwhelming. After four years, I am getting many of the wrinkles ironed out.

What do you know now that you wish you would have known when you started?

I wish I'd had the ability to say "no" or "I cannot get this done by then." I am learning to please me more.

What's the biggest mistake you've made as an at-home business owner?

My biggest mistake is not taking the time to listen, and I mean really listen, to the concerns of my family. Sometimes I pause and act like I am listening, but I am constantly thinking of other things pertaining to my businesses. My mistake is not being able to take off the business hat and put on the "mom" or "wife" hat.

What's the smartest move you've made as an at-home business owner?

Getting an accountant. I used to do all the taxes for both of my businesses, and now I don't have to worry about that aspect any longer. I wish I would have done that four years ago.

What's the most mortifying "mom moment" you've had in running your at-home business?

Having my children's friends come over (when my children still lived at home) and having all my painted stuff strewn all over the kitchen and into the family room.

What advice would you give to another woman who is interested in starting her own work-at-home business?

Trust in your feelings. Only you know what you need for yourself. Talk to your family and tell them what you are planning and why. Get a commitment from your husband and family to help you achieve your goals and achieve the balance that will need to be implemented. Then, don't be afraid of Plan B.

Learn more about Sue's business at www.studioon6th.com.

12

relying on faith to get you through

Although I saved this chapter for last in the "sanity" section, it probably should have been first. A strong faith will help you save your sanity better than anything I know—and in all areas of your life, not just as an at-home CEO. I know I could not do what I do without my faith, nor could I make it through the rough patches without the hope I have for the future.

It takes courage to be in business for oneself, and there are plenty of days when I doubt my ability, feel anxious about the future, or wonder when and how this whole "at-home" gig will come to an end. Mostly I love what I do, but sometimes I think I can't do it for another second. In those moments I cling to my favorite Bible verse: "And we know that all things work together for good to them that love God, to them who are the called according to his purpose" (Rom. 8:28 KJV). In business and in life, that's really all I need to know.

And yet, despite that assurance, at times I'm still stuck, stymied, or both in my role as president. In these times I'm comforted by knowing that I'm not alone and that I have a Chief Executive Officer above me on the organizational chart who has my back. Not only is this good from a business standpoint, but it relieves me as a mom as well. There's nothing like being in partnership with the Creator of the universe.

Many people prefer to keep their work and spiritual lives separate. But only when I began to blur the lines between the two did I hit my stride as a business owner. No, I didn't start trying to convert clients, nor am I overt about my faith. I just invited God into the office with me so that when I experience fear, face challenges that feel overwhelming, am confused about priorities, or am crushed by too many or too-tight deadlines, I am not alone. Inviting God into my work has been the most freeing experience I've had.

For me, separating work and faith is like trying to peel my shadow off the sidewalk on a sunny day: impossible. I am a spiritual person by nature. I always have been. Yet in the past I often left my spiritual side outside the office, mostly unintentionally, until I faced a particularly tough series of speaking engagements. When that happened, I prayed like never before.

And God answered like never before.

The result? Less fear. More insight. A greater appreciation for my business and how it helps provide for me and my family. A renewed partnership with the One who both created me and sustains me.

The personal growth I experienced as a result of this tough stretch of business was painful. I had to move through much anxiety and doubt to get to the other side, where a calm knowing began to infuse my work. That's how God answered: by silently speaking to my heart and telling me everything would be okay and I needed to trust his provision always, even in the face of uncertainty.

I understood that the series of engagements that led to this new knowledge was going to be tough, mostly because they were scheduled close together, which affected my preparation time. But it wasn't until I was hip deep in my pre-conference research that I discovered I was walking repeatedly into lions' dens. Infighting was tearing apart one group. Lack of trust between staff and the association members who employed them challenged another. Yet another had no clear goal for their meeting—making it difficult, if not impossible, for me to move with certainty in preparing my remarks.

I felt like a fish on land, flopping this way and that, trying to get back to the comfort of water. But even as I flopped, I realized these opportunities would grow me both personally and professionally if I would just let them. I resisted mightily but finally realized I had no choice. I was at the end of myself and needed help. That's when I got down on my knees and invited God into the picture.

For the group weakened by infighting, I designed a "truth-telling" session, something I've used since with excellent results. We simply set aside time on the program for getting things out in the open. It was an opportunity for participants to verbalize what they might not otherwise have had the courage to say. They were the things that individuals were saying privately to one another behind closed doors or whispering to one another in the hallways but didn't have permission to say out loud. I simply granted the permission. I served as the moderator as people spoke their minds. We had a couple of rules: no naming names and no pointing fingers or blaming. Simply state how you feel, then sit down.

Though this exercise was scary, I had complete calm about it. I knew it to be necessary based on God's firm voice in my heart and head. I still get nervous when I use it because audiences can be unpredictable and I don't know exactly what to expect. But each time I've used it, I've seen the benefit of getting issues out in the open.

I kept the email sent by the president of the group after the first truth-telling event. It read, "I have a summary of the evaluation forms. I have the biggest smile on my face and thought you too deserve to read something that will make your day." Though the exercise had been scary, it met the needs of audience members.

That day I learned that to be a professional speaker, I must first be a professional listener. I approach my work differently now as a result. I no longer listen just to my clients; I also listen for God's direction as I prepare for each presentation. The discipline of doing so has grown me as a professional.

The irony is that though partnership with God works beautifully, when I'm pressed for time I often forget him and head straight to the office. When I'm certain I don't have time for a morning devotion or a quick prayer, I don't try to fit one in. I know it would be easier to start the day with God rather than having to backtrack. Yet I'm always in a hurry. Always under the gun. Always looking ahead to what's next. If I could just learn to pause before diving in, I'm sure my work experience would be richer and more relaxing.

> God alone knows what types of insecurities and worries you and I wrestle with. That's why it is so freeing to invite him into partnership.

God alone knows what types of insecurities and worries you and I wrestle with. That's why it is so freeing to invite him into partnership. More than anyone else, he gets you.

He understands the pull you feel between work and family. He honors your desire to be a great wife, a fantastic mom, and an outstanding CEO. He knows how hard it is to try to grow a family and a business under one roof. He sympathizes when you feel overwhelmed and ill-equipped. In fact, the Bible tells us that he specializes in using imperfect people like us to accomplish his will.

Many times I've wondered if I should be working at all or focused solely on my household and the people in it. And yet I know I'm teaching my kids the value of hard work, the beauty of developing one's full potential, and the freedom that comes with marching to one's own beat. This isn't the life I pictured for myself when I plotted my course in high school, but it is so much richer than I could have imagined.

Though I'm a solopreneur, I don't work alone. God is at work—in me, through me, and with me. That knowledge has calmed me on more than one occasion and continues to do so as I look ahead, understanding that I'll never know enough or know it all and, best of all, that I don't have to. I know intuitively that working by faith is the best way to succeed, even as I struggle to overcome my self-reliance and my childlike desire to say, "Me do it!"

I've come to the conclusion that I often make things harder than they need to be. Author Dan Allender agrees:

> As complex as all our lives seem to be, God's plan is quite simple. He calls us to:
> - begin anywhere, and he will take us where he wants us to go;
> - start with our strengths, and he will reveal and use our weaknesses;
> - follow our desires, and he will grow his passion in us.[1]

If this truly is the case, then all we're really responsible for is beginning a task and following our desires. God, in his infinite wisdom and power, will take care of the rest.

Perhaps you attended church as a child but no longer do. Or you intend to pray but get sidetracked by your to-do list each day. (I struggle with this myself.) Or doubt makes it difficult to believe there really is a God. If that's the case, I invite you to try an experiment.

Simply ask, "God, please reveal yourself to me." It's one of the most daring sentences you'll ever speak. But don't articulate it unless you really want to see him. It's an invitation he can't and won't ignore.

David Goetz, author of *Death by Suburb*, acknowledges his own hesitation to rely on God as he developed his marketing business. Candidly, he admits:

> The first few years of my business, economic survival consumed me. I took my laptop everywhere—including our so-called family

vacation. My family suffered through my mercurial phases and an endless string of months with a dad and husband who was a grump. In many ways, the experience tapped into some darkness in me. It wasn't about economic survival only. After having done everything I could, I was simply unwilling to trust the outcome to God. I lived like an atheist.[2]

Perhaps you're already working by faith. If so, how about challenging yourself to move more deeply into partnership with God? A friend did this when she assumed control of a company after her husband became incapacitated. To signal a fresh start and a new way of operating, she asked her pastor to bless the business, similar to a house blessing. Since then she's covered the business in prayer. Watching her challenges me to do the same for my enterprise.

> When you invite God into your life and work, he shows up in amazing ways at surprising moments.

When you invite God into your life and work, he shows up in amazing ways at surprising moments. I look forward to being surprised in the future as well. This expectation adds a rich dimension to work here on earth and provides a confidence that I wouldn't otherwise have. It's truly a heavenly gift—one that makes the load of being a work-at-home mom just a little lighter.

And if you're not currently working by faith, how about giving it a try? At the minimum, I predict that you'll grow—both personally and professionally. Growth is scary. But once you're through it, the view from the other side is freeing. Plus, there's something wonderful about turning the future, both good and bad, fully over to the One who can see it before we can even imagine it.

Lesson Learned: It's not necessary to leave faith out of your entrepreneurial life. Doing so denies you access to powerful insights and the confidence necessary for building a successful business.

Work-at-Home Mom Profile

Amy Peterson

Name and type of business:

The Closet Guy, Inc. Closet installation and professional organizing services.

How long have you been in business?

The business started in September 2002. I began working for the company in June 2006.

Why did you choose this business?

I chose to work with my husband because I love to organize, be organized, and help people organize. My husband and I actually stumbled upon Closet Maid dealer information in August 2002. I took over the duties my husband previously handled so that he can focus more time and energy on what he does best—design and build custom closets. I love working with our customers, and I am so happy when I call them to follow up and they say that now they have twice the space they had before!

What's the toughest part of running a business and family under one roof?

The toughest part is saying yes to everything *but* work. I have three children. Currently two are in school and one is in preschool two mornings a week. If I volunteer for all the activities at my kids' schools, go on all the field trips, volunteer at church or in the community, watch kids for friends, schedule mom and child playdates, do housework, and more, the business work does not get done. I have had to discipline myself in scheduling time to work and then honoring the time that I set aside to work. I also have had to set aside time for my family that is "their" time and not just mom multitasking, trying to get everything done. It is a daily challenge.

What unique child care strategies have you used to enable you to work successfully from home?

This has been a learning experience for me. Summers especially are hard! So far I have two summers under my belt since I started working from home, and I did not have much of a plan for either. We played a lot, and as a result our business suffered in the fall. This summer I am working on a plan.

What's your favorite part of being in business for yourself?

I love the flexibility (yet that is also my most challenging part!). I love working 150 percent for a company that I am directly a part of. I have always worked really hard for other people, so it is great to work hard for our business and reap the rewards.

What's your least favorite part?

It is frustrating when you work really hard and think you are doing all the right things, but you still struggle to make ends meet. I pay the bills for our business as well as pay all the bills for our home, and sometimes that task wears on me. When business is slow and money is tight, I feel frustrated. Things always seem to turn around, but it still wears on me.

What do you know now that you wish you would have known when you started?

How challenging it is to balance home and work. It took me about a year and a half to get the hang of working from home because I didn't take it seriously at first. I said yes to so many people and seemed to put our business last. I felt guilty telling people I had to work. When you work from home, people don't seem to take you seriously.

What's the biggest mistake you've made as an at-home business owner?

Probably not sitting down with a small business adviser in the beginning. We never put together a business plan. We never applied for a small business loan; we just borrowed money from my husband's dad, got training on how to build and design closets, and away we went! We have learned some things the hard way. We could have saved a lot of time and money had we started off working with an adviser.

What's the smartest move you've made as an at-home business owner?

Hiring professionals to handle things beyond our expertise, like an accountant, attorney, graphic designer, web designer, and marketing consultant. We love to build, design, and organize closets. That is what we do best. We can handle the other basics of running the business, but some things are just beyond our expertise.

What's the most mortifying "mom moment" you've had in running your at-home business?

The only thing I can think of is that my daughter has drawn on some of our furniture because she was left in the living room watching a video while I was working. Now we have black permanent marker all over our ottoman!

What advice would you give to another woman who is interested in starting her own work-at-home business?

Seek advice from a small business adviser. Get your papers in order and keep track of receipts. Since I am an organizer, I would also recommend that you set up a designated space in the home for your "work" and keep all work stuff in that area. Set up files for receipts, bills, and important paperwork. If you set up a system before starting your business, you are more likely to follow up with it.

Learn more about The Closet Guy, Inc., at www.theclosetguyinc.com.

preserving your profit

13

accepting the at-home ceo mantle

As we launch into the second half of this book and transition from saving your sanity to preserving your profit, it's appropriate to focus on how you think of yourself and how your thoughts determine your effectiveness.

How *do* you think of yourself? As the CEO of your business? Or simply as a mom who works from home? The difference is crucial.

As your business grows, the decisions you have to make become more complex and far-reaching. Often I've been intimidated, overwhelmed, and paralyzed when it comes to the choices I have. I feel pressed for time, fearful I don't have the right knowledge, and hampered by my lack of experience in excelling in all areas of running a successful enterprise. I used to let these feelings and fears limit me. No more.

I've benefited from a valuable piece of advice I heard well before I became an entrepreneur. Simply stated, it's this: *act like the person you want to be.*

In your opinion, what characteristics does a successful at-home entrepreneur possess? Courage? Vision? Creativity? Flexibility? The ability to multitask effectively? Take a minute to make a list.

Once your list is complete, you can begin to act *as if* you possess these characteristics. And the more you act as if you have them, the more quickly you will develop them so that you truly do possess them. In their book *The Experience Economy*, Joseph Pine II and James Gilmore write:

> Many acting teachers since have parlayed the notion into a formal acting technique called "As If." Says one such instructor, Michael Kearns, "Acting *as if* is a great technique to apply to real life. As obnoxious as it sounds, it's a bit like positive thinking. You're at a party, feeling glum and determined to have a lousy time. Sometimes an adjustment—acting as if you're having the time of your life—will actually alter your mood, allowing you to look at the occasion through a different filter."[1]

How does this work in business? When you face a tough decision in your business ask, *How would a CEO of a large corporation make this decision, and how do I need to act as if I had these same abilities?* Make a list of the steps the CEO would take. Then act *as if* you were that person and follow the steps you outlined. The more you do this, the more the process will become second nature and the more likely you are to develop the skills you don't currently have. It's an essential part of accepting the CEO mantle.

Though you may not have the same skills and knowledge as the CEO of a large company, you don't need to. You simply need to act *as if* you do. They don't always have all the answers either. When they don't, they use their resources to find the answers they seek. As an at-home CEO who desires success, you must do the same. This may require a change in your perception of yourself. If and when you catch yourself thinking *I'm just a work-at-home mom* when you are faced with a challenge that isn't easily solved, add the words, *as well as an at-home CEO.*

Do you see how empowering it is to move from "just a work-at-home mom" to "at-home CEO"? The shift in thinking, though subtle, is powerful. How you think about yourself ultimately determines your level of success. This is true not only in your work life but in your professional life as well.

How you think about yourself ultimately determines your level of success.

CEOs are "can" thinkers rather than "can't" thinkers. When faced with a dilemma, they believe they can solve it. To do so, they ask themselves three questions:

- What do I know about this situation?
- What don't I know?
- What don't I know that I need to know?

The last question is perhaps the most important. It's this question that drives CEOs. And it's this question that will help you act like a CEO, even when you don't feel like one.

Acting like the person you want to be in business will enable you to:

- obtain the information you need to make necessary decisions for your business
- persevere in making sales calls to meet your sales quota each month
- rethink your business when necessary to make it more satisfying for you
- prioritize so that you are working as efficiently as possible and are able to meet the demands of growing a business and a family under one roof
- determine when it's time to take a break so you don't get burned out or lose interest entirely
- say no to projects that don't interest you, won't be profitable, or are more trouble than they are worth
- create boundaries so your business life doesn't spill into your personal life in a negative way

- develop the wisdom you need over time to grow your business effectively

When you believe you can be successful as CEO, you will be. If you don't think you can, you won't be. The choice is yours, and it's directly related to how you see yourself.

When you act like the person you aspire to be, you're more likely to become that person. When you act *as if* you have the characteristics you desire, eventually you'll develop them. These two ideas are powerful when it comes to both your personal and professional growth.

> Act as if you have what it takes to make your enterprise successful, and you'll be more likely to be a success.

Your thoughts determine your reality. When you see yourself as the president and/or CEO of your business, with all the attendant responsibility and authority, you'll be more likely to act as if you're the chief executive officer. It takes CEO thinking to get your business to the next level and make it as profitable as possible. Act as if you have what it takes to make your enterprise successful, and you'll be more likely to be a success.

Profitability isn't outside of you. It starts in your head and your heart. Wise entrepreneurs know this, and they nurture their self-image and self-esteem accordingly. Don't let anyone tell you that you can't. You're a CEO, and CEOs are "can" thinkers. From this day forward, stop yourself whenever you say or think the words "I can't." Rephrase the statement so that it's a "can" statement. Act like the person you want to be, and act *as if* you have what it takes. If you can master this advice, you'll be well on your way to profitability.

Lesson Learned: Act like the person you want to be, and you'll develop the courage, skills, and knowledge necessary to run your business successfully, even while mothering your children.

Work-at-Home Mom Profile

Betsy Walter

Name and type of business:
Circle of Song-Buckhold Music, a music publisher.

How long have you been in business?
Since July 1996.

Why did you choose this business?
I am a songwriter and music is in my heart. I enjoy the creation of both the song and the demo recording of the song.

What's the toughest part of running a business and a family under one roof?
Keeping from being interrupted by the children, especially when I am writing and in the creative mode.

What unique child care strategies have you used to enable you to work successfully from home?
I have to have child care. I use a nanny part time so that I may work on Monday, Wednesday, and Friday usually. Also, the children go to Mom's Day Out programs, preschool, and elementary school.

What's your favorite part of being in business for yourself?
Getting to pursue my love of music and being creative. It is my creative outlet.

What's your least favorite part?
Wearing the publisher hat instead of the songwriter hat. I have to keep track of what artists or film/TV music supervisors are looking for music and make appropriate pitches. Then, of course, I have to follow up consistently on the pitches I have made. This all takes away from my very limited time for songwriting and producing.

What's the smartest move you've made as an at-home business owner?

Securing child care.

What's the most mortifying "mom moment" you've had in running your at-home business?

Probably having to catch my daughter as she was falling out of her high chair while I was on a voice-activated phone call. Her scream and my catch made the voice say, "Did you say New Jersey?"

What advice would you give to another woman who is interested in starting her own work-at-home business?

You have to secure consistent child care. And you have to have a location inside your home that can be away from the kids' view and noises.

Learn more about Betsy's music at
http://www.broadjam.com/artists/home.php?artistID=10559.

14

professional (and other) advice

you don't have to know it all to be a success

Though CEOs are "can" thinkers, they also understand it's not humanly possible to know everything they need to know to run a profitable company. They embrace the fact that, as James Champey and Nitin Nohria wrote, "No solo ruler of a complex company can ever have enough creativity, knowledge, and time to make the right decisions single-handedly. His or her survival depends on sowing and reaping the brilliant work of others."[1]

You will face times in your entrepreneurial life when you'll need to seek out the advice of others. It may be free advice from colleagues, friends, and family, or it may be advice you pay for such as that from accountants, attorneys, or a professional coach. How do you know when to seek help?

Seek help when you're stuck. It's a good idea to pick up the phone and talk to someone you trust and respect anytime you're stuck. Outline your challenge, your options, and why you're having trouble moving ahead. Then just listen. Often hearing another person respond to your dilemma will enable you to see things in a new light and help identify a "next step" for you. Taking just one "next step" will often allow you to overcome inertia, get unstuck, and begin rolling again.

You don't have to know everything you're going to do or the order you're going to do it in. You simply have to figure out one step to take to start moving again. This is true in your personal life as well as your professional life and is a tenet to remember any time you find yourself sidelined by paralysis.

Seek help when you don't have the necessary knowledge. Sometimes being stuck is the result of not having the right knowledge to make the decisions you need to make. When you know you lack knowledge and you're able to specifically identify the know-how you're missing, it's much easier to figure out whom you need to talk to. Are you facing a tax or record-keeping question? You likely need to talk to an accountant. Do you need a contract reviewed? Call an attorney. Want to know how to set up an online store? Call a web designer. Do you need help being held accountable? Find a personal coach.

If you can't afford the services of a professional, consider bartering. Recently I was able to get a new logo and design for my website because I was willing to help a designer look at her current operations and determine how she could make them more effective. If you choose this option, be sure to capture your agreement in writing so there will be no misunderstanding regarding what you're trading. In addition, be aware there are tax consequences for bartering.

Seek help when you're conflicted and/or lack clarity. Sometimes identifying a "next step" isn't difficult at all. It's prioritizing *which* next step you should take that may be agonizing. When you feel conflicted or lack clear direction regarding what's next in your business, it's good to turn to others who can offer a fresh perspective. Having a network of people with whom you can talk things through is important, especially for at-home entrepreneurs who live and work in the same environment and don't always have a change of scenery to challenge their thinking or shake things up.

I'm a big fan of the value of learning from other people. But where can you find people from whom to seek advice? Joining groups of people who do what you do or know what you want to know is a great way to shorten your learning curve. By meeting other people and learning about their areas of expertise, it's easy to develop an informal network you can turn to when you're in need of counsel. Here's how to find a group that's right for you:

Ask around. As you meet and work with other self-employed people, ask them which groups they belong to and which are the most beneficial to them as entrepreneurs.

Watch your local paper. Check out the business calendar and events section of your local newspaper to learn about organizations in your area. There truly is an association for everything. By watching the paper, you'll find out which groups meet locally, and you might discover some you didn't previously know existed!

Attend as a guest. Most groups will allow you to attend a meeting or two as a guest. That way you can catch a sense of what the group's about and whether or not it's a good fit for you before you pay membership dues.

Once you join, become involved. The quickest way to meet other people in an association is to volunteer on a committee or on the leadership team. Doing so gives you broad exposure. In addition, you'll learn about membership benefits and opportunities more rapidly by virtue of your involvement.

Identify what you hope to learn or gain from membership, then find a group that meets this need. If you'd like to learn to be a better public speaker, consider Toastmasters. If you want to learn more about event planning, join a group of meeting professionals.

If you're in sales and want to improve your skills in that arena, you might consider the National Association of Sales Professionals. (You can even find narrowly focused sales groups such as the Association of Timeshare Sales Professionals and the American Association of Pharmaceutical Sales Professionals!)

Hang out with people who do what you do. As a speaker and association consultant, I'm a member of both the National Speakers Association and the American Society of Association Executives. As a writer, I'm a member of the Advanced Writers and Speakers Association. I've always been amazed at how generous people who can be considered competitors are with their knowledge and experience. My learning curve has been shortened tremendously by this generosity. It was especially helpful as I was getting my feet wet and learning the ropes as a new speaker and writer. By learning from others' experience, I've managed to avoid many mistakes I know I would have made.

If you're a member of a network marketing team, take advantage of the friendships you make at meetings and participate fully in any teleconferences or web seminars offered by the company. In addition, utilize your upline as a valuable source of advice.

Use the Internet. Search engines make it easier than ever to locate organizations that may be helpful to you. I'm a fan of the National Association of Women Business Owners (check to see if a chapter meets in your local area) and have heard good things about the benefits offered by the National Association for the Self-Employed, which includes affordable health insurance and discounts on supplies.

Another valuable form of networking is available online, since likeminded individuals are now meeting in chat rooms and via email loops to discuss topics in a convenient forum. I subscribe to three feeds that deliver conversation and connection to my inbox each morning. I've previewed more than these three over the years but have a strict policy of only keeping subscriptions to those that are most helpful. Otherwise I'd spend all day reading and wouldn't write a word myself!

Regardless of what group you join or how you find it, it's essential you have a way to sharpen your mind, hone your skills, and challenge your thinking to be as profitable as possible in your business.

A smart CEO knows that at times she will have the necessary knowledge and skills to make informed decisions. She also knows that at times she will need to seek advice. Surround yourself with a wide network of people *before* you need guidance, and you'll be more likely to have access to the counsel you need when you need it, rather than having to begin a prolonged search.

> Surround yourself with a wide network of people *before* you need guidance, and you'll be more likely to have access to the counsel you need when you need it.

Smart CEOs don't fly solo. Instead they remain involved in the associations that offer the most in terms of personal and professional growth. They know they can cut their learning curve by hanging out with others who do what they do and know what they need and want to know.

Take a minute to assess where you are in regard to your own affiliations and at-home responsibilities. Is this something you've let slide as you work to manage both a business and your family? Because lack of time is an issue for many at-home entrepreneurs, memberships are often the first to go when one experiences a time crunch. If you've let all your memberships lapse, consider adding one back into your schedule this year. Or if you're a member of too many groups and haven't been able to attend meetings or get involved with any of them more intimately, consider resigning from some and focusing on the ones that most closely match your needs at this time. This will enable you to receive the biggest bang for your buck.

If memberships just aren't in the picture for you right now due to your child care obligations, consider subscribing to the association publications that will be the most helpful to you. Doing so allows you to stay abreast of changes and information that will help you in your business as well as learn about valuable educational opportunities you can attend as a nonmember. Monitoring association activities in this manner will keep you in the loop without the full expense or time commitment of membership. As your children mature and their needs become less demanding, you'll likely have the opportunity to rejoin the groups you found to be most beneficial in the past.

You don't have to spend an inordinate amount of time networking for the concept to be helpful. One group I meet with is simply comprised of two other moms who work from home as writers. We get together several times a year to compare notes, sympathize with one another, and celebrate our successes. In between the face-to-face meetings, we email and call when appropriate. Though not formally organized, this group has been one of the best for me in terms of helping me understand the challenges of working as a writer from a home office.

Though time is at a premium for work-at-home moms, it's important to network with others as you're able. Doing so helps keep your skills sharp and provides you with a valuable trove of experience and resources that come in handy when you're stuck or need access to expertise you don't possess. Remember, you don't have to know it all to be a success. You simply have to know where to go to find the information you need to successfully run, and grow, your business.

Lesson Learned: Smart entrepreneurs don't fly solo. Instead, they actively develop friendships and professional relationships that will allow them to secure the counsel they need before they need it.

Work-at-Home Mom Profile

Dana Saal

Name and type of business:

Meeting Works, offering convention and conference planning services.

How long have you been in business?

Eight years.

Why did you choose this business?

It was my career when I worked full-time at an association.

What's the toughest part of running a business and a family under one roof?

The interruptions during busy times—work invading my family and family invading my work. This is the case with working outside the home, of course, but the pull to be in both places at once is even greater for a home-based business because you can't walk away from it as easily. Because there is no physical separation, there is no mental separation.

What unique child care strategies have you used to enable you to work successfully from home?

I started my home-based business when my children were in first grade, so I haven't had to use child care while I am at home working. However, I am most productive during the day when they are at school. They have always been good at entertaining themselves while I worked. In addition, they understood that I couldn't talk with them when I was on the phone.

Traveling creates its own challenges. In addition to my husband helping, I've hired high school girls to drive my daughters to their after-school activities. For my long trips (six to eight days), relatives would stay at our house when the girls were young.

What's your favorite part of being in business for yourself?

Being here for my family. My husband loves the arrangement, especially since my girls are talkers. I can stop and listen whenever they are in the mood to chat, vent, or ask. He misses the fact that he doesn't hear the conversations firsthand, but he's thrilled I'm here to listen and then relate them to him. A close second is that I don't have to deal with office politics.

What's your least favorite part?

It never goes away. I use my office for personal work (paying bills, using the computer) so there are times when I just want to leave. It makes it tough to sit down and pay bills because I don't want to be in that room!

What do you know now that you wish you would have known when you started?

That I could have done it earlier.

What's the biggest mistake you've made as an at-home business owner?

Underpricing and "scope creep," which is assuming responsibility for tasks not included in my contract and therefore that I am not compensated for.

What's the smartest move you've made as an at-home business owner?

Making the decision to work from home. It has been a blessing for our family.

What's the most mortifying "mom moment" you've had in running your at-home business?

I've been lucky; I don't have mortifying moments (or I'm not easily mortified!). One awkward phone call popped in my head when I read the question. I was on the phone with a longtime colleague when the girls started shrieking at each other and slamming doors. I knew they were mad and not in distress, so I acknowledged the commotion to the caller and said I would handle it and then call her back. She understood.

What advice would you give to another woman who is interested in starting her own work-at-home business?

I have never had to market my business. All my work has come from word of mouth and spin-offs. In other words, I have been able to focus on being a meeting professional, not a marketer. So my advice is that a woman starting a business without connections in the industry needs to take into account the extra effort and financial impact that might be required to simply get off the ground. I think that added dimension would affect the whole experience.

15

the tax man comes

record-keeping and deductions

Once you've accepted the CEO mantle and developed a network or list of resources, you should turn your attention to your finances since they are a concrete measure of your success.

I am not an accountant. But it doesn't take an accounting degree to know that keeping accurate records is an important part of a healthy business. Your financial record-keeping will help you determine your profit (and the resulting taxes) and provide a snapshot of your effectiveness as you monitor income and spending. It's also an important way to gauge if you've priced your goods and services profitably. The better your system, the easier reporting will be and the better your grasp on all things money related. We'll discuss both record-keeping and deductions in this chapter.

The number one rule for moms who work at home is this: do not mingle your personal and business finances. Open a separate checking account for your business. And, if necessary, secure a separate credit card so that you can keep your personal and business-related expenses separate. Deposit all of your income in the checking account. Pay all of your expenses out of the business checking account or with your business credit card (to be a wise steward of your money, be sure you pay it off monthly). Then at the end of the year you'll have an accurate record of income and expenses.

Check with your bank before you open your checking account. They may require proof that you've filed a "Doing Business As" form with your local or county government. Your banker may also be able to alert you to other regulations specific to your area.

> The number one rule for moms who work at home is this: do not mingle your personal and business finances.

I personally believe it's essential to stay on top of your business finances on a monthly basis. Though this is not my favorite chore, I use a simple software program to track income and spending. I can compare this year's figures to last year's to find out how I'm doing as well as monitor my year-to-date performance. Many easy-to-use software programs (such as Quicken and Quick-Books) are on the market to make it possible for business owners to track and access their financial data.

In addition to inputting my figures, I take time to organize my expense receipts each month. It takes less than a half hour to file them, but doing so ensures that my end-of-year tax preparation will run smoothly. Plus, I'll have necessary proof if I'm ever audited.

Once your record-keeping is in order, you should take the time to learn what's allowable as an expense deduction for you as a self-employed individual. The more you deduct, the less your profit. The less your profit, the less you pay in taxes. The less you pay in taxes, the more you keep for yourself.

According to the Internal Revenue Service, "To be deductible, a business expense must be both ordinary and necessary. An ordinary expense is one that is common and accepted in your field of business. A necessary expense is one that is appropriate and helpful for your business. An expense does not have to be indispensable to be considered necessary."

The challenge in determining what's deductible is that it differs based on occupation. Day care providers can write off the cost of toys they buy for their charges, while authors can deduct the cost of books purchased for review, critique, and craft development.

June Walker, tax and financial adviser to self-employed people, contends that a deductible business expense may be anything you do that has a relationship to your work, adds to your skills, nourishes your business creativity, boosts your chances of making a sale, garners you recognition, or promotes your business. June further advises that every self-employed person develop an independent business mind-set by considering that each time she writes a check, reaches into her wallet for money, or presents a credit or debit card, she may be transacting business and therefore able to deduct all, or a portion, of the cost.[1]

June, the author of *Self-Employed Tax Solutions*, was kind enough to grant me permission to share the following list of deductible expenses with you. It's an excellent resource for at-home CEOs and is available online at www.junewalkeronline.com.

1. Advertising/Promotion
- Business cards
- Christmas/holiday cards
- Mailing lists
- Newspaper ads
- Photos, film, and processing
- Posters
- Professional registries
- Résumés
- CDs and DVDs about you or your business
- Website development and hosting

2. Auto/Truck/Motorcycle

3. Commissions and Fees
- Agent fees paid
- Franchise fees

4. Sub-Contractor Fees
- Assistant
- Models
- Singing coach
- Supervision for psychologists
- Typist

5. Equipment (costs more than $200 and lasts more than one year)
- Office furniture
- Computer, printer, all technical hardware
- Washer, dryer for a massage therapist (business percentage if used for personal as well)
- Alarm system
- Camera and accessories
- File cabinets
- Lamps, rugs
- Music system
- Stand-alone shelves
- TV/VCR/DVD

6. Business Insurance
- Business interruption
- Disability—for non-spousal employees only
- Fire and theft
- Liability
- Malpractice
- Workers' compensation for employees

7. **Business Loan Interest**
   - Mortgage on business property
   - Business portion of credit card finance charges

8. **Legal and Professional Services**—must be for business services; e.g., not will preparation
   - Accountant fees
   - Attorney fees
   - Bookkeeper fees
   - Lobbying expenses (with restrictions)
   - Pension administrator fees

9. **Supplies**—general supplies used in your office or workplace
   - Office materials: e.g., paper, toner, lightbulbs
   - Cleaning supplies and paper products: e.g., tissues, towels
   - Coffee, bottled water, hard candy for clients
   - Fire extinguisher
   - Flowers or plants for the office
   - Software

10. **Postage**
    - Stamps
    - FedEx, UPS
    - Freight
    - Messenger service
    - Post office box (business percentage if used for personal as well)

11. **Equipment Rental or Lease**
    - Chairs
    - Copier
    - Workshop tools

12. Rent on Business Property
- Office
- Studio
- Rehearsal space
- Warehouse

13. Repairs/Maintenance
- Of equipment: e.g., piano tuning, service contract
- Of the office: e.g., cleaning service, repair of a window
- Laundering of linens used in your practice

14. Supplies (incidental supplies used in your specific business, not office supplies and not supplies used in the production of your product)
- Animal treats for a dog sitter
- Linens for a massage therapist
- Music scores for a music teacher
- Props and scripts for a performing artist

15. Business Taxes
- Employer's share of payroll taxes
- Federal highway use tax
- Franchise tax
- Gross receipts or sales tax
- NY unincorporated business tax
- Personal property tax on business assets
- Real estate tax on business property
- Zoning permit

16. Licenses and Fees
- Yearly business license
- Franchise fees
- Regulatory fees to state and local governments

17. Travel
- Airfare
- Parking
- Cabs
- Lodging
- Mileage reimbursement

18. Meals/Entertainment
- With business associates: e.g., clients, potential clients, colleagues, employees
- At your office
- At a sporting or entertainment event
- Parties for business associates
- For the general public: e.g., for a grand opening, gallery show

19. Telephone and Other Communication Utilities
- Monthly service and accessories for business line
- Business percentage of personal line—excluding base line charge
- Cell phone
- Answering service
- Pager
- Internet service provider

20. Office or Studio Utilities (not home office)
- Electricity, heat, water
- Exterminator service
- Security company monthly fee
- Trash pickup

21. Wages to Employees

22. Bank Services Charges (if account is both personal and business, then you must allocate accordingly)
- Business bank account fees
- Check printing fees
- Client returned check fee
- Safe deposit box

23. Copyright Fees/Royalties/Patents

24. Costumes/Cleaning/Makeup
- Tuxedo/evening dress
- Hair done for award presentation
- Makeup for a performer
- Uniforms—clothing with the business name on it

25. Dues/Entrance Fees
- Civic and public service organizations: e.g., chambers of commerce
- Competition fees
- Museums
- Professional societies: e.g., bar or medical associations, real estate boards

26. Business Gifts (maximum $25 per person, per year)
- To clients
- To potential clients
- To business associates
- Thank you to mom for fixing your computer
- Tips: e.g., for travel assistants, backstage help

27. Studio/Office in the Home
- Prorated percentage of mortgage
- Prorated percentage of utilities

28. Photocopies/Printing

29. Publications—anything you read related to your business
- Books
- Magazines
- Newspapers
- Newsletter subscriptions

30. Recording Costs

31. Study/Education/Seminars/Research
- Cable TV
- Classes
- Concerts
- Conventions
- Document gathering
- Galleries
- Lessons
- Library fee
- Movies
- Museums
- Performances
- Tuition and fees
- Videos/DVDs (purchase or rental)
- Workshops

32. Public Transportation
- Bus
- Subway
- Taxi
- Train

33. Supplies Used in the Production of Your Product

If you're interested in learning more about deductible expenses, consider picking up a copy of June's *Self-Employed Tax Solutions*. It's an excellent resource, as is June's website at www.junewalker online.com. Her blog is worth subscribing to if you're interested in learning how to keep more of what you make.

If you're uncertain as to whether something is deductible, check with your personal tax adviser. And if you don't have one, hire one. (You may notice this piece of advice is common in the "Work-at-Home Mom Profiles.")

Here's how to make the most of your deductions:

Know what's deductible. Study the list above so you know what's deductible and which receipts you should keep. You may be surprised by what you can write off. For example, if you conduct business on the way to or from your family vacation, you may be able to write off a portion of your travel expenses. Mileage for in-town business-related trips is also deductible, as is a second phone line if it's used for business.

If in doubt, ask. This is where a tax reference book or a good accountant comes in. While it may be easier *not* to ask, doing so may well cost you money that would be better invested in your retirement account or a child's college fund.

Realize that small deductions add up. My bank is 5.6 miles away. With the current IRS standard mileage deduction of 50.5 cents per mile (for 2008), every trip to the bank for a business-related transaction results in a deduction of $2.83 (50.5 cents x 5.6 miles). Last year alone my mileage deduction totaled $1,971. (I record each trip in a mileage log to provide documentation for the IRS.) Remember, deductions decrease taxable income, and lower taxable income means paying less tax.

Keep your receipts. Develop a simple record-keeping system that's easy to use. You'll need to keep your records for seven years after the relevant tax return is filed. (Though the receipts only need to be kept temporarily, you should keep your tax returns forever.)

If you need help developing a working system for record-keeping, get it. Though record-keeping and taxes can be tedious, they represent an area in which solopreneurs can make a huge difference in their bottom line. You owe it to yourself and your family to excel in this area. If you're intimidated or uncertain in this regard, make a commitment to learn what you need to know starting today.

Lesson Learned: Smart entrepreneurs are both technically savvy and financially savvy—and if they aren't, they should partner with someone who is!

16

the right equipment

ensuring you have the tools you need

There's never been a better time to be in business for yourself. Between personal computers, email, and cell phones, you can work cost effectively anywhere you want. In addition, scanners, fax machines, binding machines, and laminators are inexpensive. It's possible to begin a business with a small investment and to have a fully operational office relatively easily.

I wish I would have realized this when I first started working from home.

Many moms have a tendency to worry excessively about income versus expense when they begin their at-home enterprise. Because they don't want their businesses to be a financial drain on the household, they are careful about expenditures, which is wise. But sometimes equipment purchases are necessary. The right equipment may help you become profitable faster, which may require swallowing hard and investing in the right tools for your business.

My daughter was two and my son was in an infant carrier when I began my life as a work-at-home mom. I remember bundling them both up to brave nasty winter weather to go to the local pharmacy or library to make author copies of the journal I edited to send to contributors. After the copies were made, I'd come home and individually package each article in a FedEx envelope, then send it for approval. Though the overnight service was a godsend, I still had to complete many steps to get the final version of an article in the hands of its author.

Now, of course, with email and portable data files, I'm able to send an article immediately, even to far-flung countries, which I often do since the publication I work with is international. I'm still amazed that I can communicate with Scotland in just a few seconds via my computer. But I digress.

After one particularly difficult trip with the children (I was on deadline, after all!), I began to wonder about the cost of a personal photocopier that would allow me to make copies from the comfort of my home office rather than having to continually venture out with my children in tow. Until that time, I had focused on maximizing my income and minimizing expenses. If there was a way to save money, I was going to do it. The only problem was, it caused me a lot of frustration simply because getting myself and two children bundled up and out the door wasn't always the easiest thing, especially since my daughter was potty training. Inevitably, we'd be ready to walk out the door and I'd hear, "I have to go potty." Though it had taken me a good fifteen minutes to get everyone into their outerwear and to ensure I had what I needed to photocopy, I'd internally sigh due to the delay and we'd take off our coats, march to the bathroom—and wait. Sometimes, it didn't take long, but other times I'd have to read her a couple of books before the task was completed. Then we'd bundle up again.

One particular day remains in my memory. It was windy and cold with freezing rain, but duty called, so off we went. The streets were hazardous, and I knew I shouldn't be out. But the weatherman was calling for even worse weather ahead, and I felt that if I didn't get the work done that day, I might really get behind in the production schedule. So I persisted.

I can picture how I must have looked, escorting both children out of the car, holding a two-year-old's hand, hefting an infant, and trying to protect my original documents from the driving rain. The ice made it difficult to walk, so I shuffled my feet delicately to remain standing and not take a fall. I urged my daughter to "hurry up" so we could get inside the building quicker. It was tedious to have to do my work with young, dependent children around. It certainly wasn't like the old days when I went to the office, had an assistant to help me, and enjoyed the luxury of paid sick days. I was on my own now, and that day, more than ever, I realized it.

In retrospect, I know if I had had a photocopier in my office, it would have taken me less than ten minutes to complete the above task. Instead, it took nearly an hour. Not a wise use of time. In fact, this event pushed me over the edge. When the weather cleared up, I went to the local office supply store to price photocopiers. At the time they cost several hundred dollars. I knew I would never make enough copies to make the per-copy price equivalent with the library price of ten cents per copy. But I also knew the ten cents per copy price didn't reflect the amount of time and angst it cost to get the job done. It was time to buck up.

In retrospect, I realize I was waiting for encouragement from my husband to spend the money. I'd drop hints like, "It sure is difficult to get everyone out the door to get photocopies made," and "It really isn't a wise use of my time to have to leave the house every time I need a photocopy." Though my husband heard me, he hadn't witnessed what it was like to literally try to juggle kids and papers to accomplish some of my work. Though I was waiting for permission, I finally realized I'd have to bite the bullet and make the decision myself. It's part of being a CEO.

Making my first major purchase for my business was freeing. I saw I could spend money wisely in a way that would make me more effective, and I wouldn't go broke. Since then I've made a purchase each year that enables me to save time or work more effectively.

One of the reasons I was hesitant to invest in equipment was that I didn't know how much future work to expect. Because my work was initially per project, it was difficult to gauge the sustainability of my business. At the time I never dreamed that once I started, I'd still be at it a decade later! As I shared previously, I can see that my early at-home attitude affected my ability to be decisive and to act like the wise CEO I wanted to be. If you're early in your at-home career, you can decide to take the bull by the horns and move with more authority than I first did.

Time has a way of bringing things into focus. As I write, I can't believe I agonized so much over buying a photocopier. It seems ludicrous today, especially since now you can buy a reliable one for under $100. But at the time, I confused being successful with being profitable and kept my eye tightly on the bottom line. Though I still pay attention to income and expenses, I now see the value of something my father taught me in my teens: *it takes money to make money.*

When a large expenditure is necessary, I remind myself of this fact. It makes it easier to invest in my business. The following ideas also help me:

Create a regular schedule for making purchases and upgrades necessary to support your business. I find that December is an excellent time to invest in the equipment I need for my business. First, I have an idea what my profit will be for the year just passed. By investing some of this profit, I can reduce my tax burden and ensure I have what I need. Second, it's often possible to find the items I need at a reduced price due to holiday sales. Though it's sometimes hard to justify spending money because we're also making Christmas gift purchases at the same time, it makes financial sense to do so.

Pay attention to what frustrates you. My current computer is five years old. Though it doesn't seem old to me, the newer models are computing faster, have more storage capability, and can run more programs simultaneously. Lately, my system has been sluggish and takes longer to process my requests. I've noticed that I'm sighing impatiently a lot while I'm waiting for what I need. I'm beginning to see that a new computer may, in fact, be on my list for next year. I don't like it. I don't want to spend the money. But I realize that to be able to work as quickly and effectively as possible, an upgrade is necessary. Paying attention to what frustrates you is a good way to identify where your next investments should be.

Image is everything. Equipment isn't the only area where you may need to spend money. I recently swallowed hard and hired a professional web designer to redo my website. As I surfed the Net and visited other sites, I began to notice that my site looked dated. Plus, I didn't have the ability to make changes myself. Though I know I could have found someone to do it for less, I chose instead to select the firm that would be able to meet my current goals and help position me for the next decade. (If you want to see the result, please visit me online at www.making workathomework.com.)

> Paying attention to what frustrates you is a good way to identify where your next investments should be.

While it was tough to make the investment, I focused on the fact that it takes money to make money. Nowadays it's possible to design your own website for under $100. Depending on your line of work, this may be sufficient for you. But you have to ask yourself if doing so is really the best representation of your business.

I knew that to take my business to the next level, I needed the help of skilled web professionals. While we were updating the site, it made sense to develop a new logo and new look as well. Expensive? Yes. Scary? Definitely. Worth it? Absolutely. Above all, this investment shows my clients I'm serious about my business and worth what I charge.

What types of image-related investments do you need to make? A logo? Business cards? Professional marketing materials? Take a step back and ask yourself what you're missing that would help you convey to customers that you're serious about your business. Then invest accordingly.

Don't be a martyr. I resisted making the jump to cable Internet for as long as I could, due to the cost. Dial-up was less than half of what I'd pay for cable, and I was determined to use my money wisely. But remaining with dial-up meant waiting excessively for photos or documents to download. As an editor, sometimes I'd receive several things simultaneously, resulting in disconnection or an afternoon that was entirely wasted as I waited for a download to finish. Now that I've upgraded, I can't imagine running my business the old way. Though I'm not the first to invest in new technology or equipment, my goal is also not to be the last.

Consider charging customers to help recover the cost of equipment purchases. Some professional speakers I know charge a materials fee to cover the cost of providing handouts for their programs. By doing so they are able to recoup some of their equipment cost. If you're in the type of business where this idea would work comfortably for you, adapt it accordingly. Perhaps a materials or operations fee would enable you to secure and maintain the equipment you need more readily.

Realize that investments can and should include education as well as equipment. If you buy a new piece of software but don't know how to use it to its fullest extent, you won't achieve the maximum benefit from it. As you plan equipment investments, be sure to give yourself the gift of necessary education as well. On the other hand, if you don't need to know every nuance of a piece of software, rather than investing in intensive training, find someone who uses it regularly and ask them to teach you only what you want to know. I have a friend who bought QuickBooks but didn't want to learn how to use the program in its entirety. She wanted to know only enough to be able to run her income and expenses on a monthly basis. She hired a local bookkeeper to come to her office, set up the program, and teach her what she needed to know to be able to record her income and expenses each month and run a report. She accomplished all this for less than a couple hundred dollars.

If you're a mom at home, you may or may not have money to invest in your business. You may have started it on a shoestring and continue operating it on a shoestring. Regardless, I've learned the hard way that sometimes "saving money" really is shortsighted.

"Saving money" sometimes means you don't have the equipment you need to do your job efficiently and effectively.

"Saving money" sometimes means you can't charge as much as you're worth. I'm appalled at some of the marketing materials I used early in my freelance life and learned a valuable lesson after I paid to have more professional resources designed. When I looked more professional on paper and online, I felt more professional, giving me the confidence I needed to increase my fees, which I hadn't done in years. Now that I've taken another step in this direction with my recent logo and website redesign, I'll again review my fees.

"Saving money" sometimes means your work is harder than it has to be, your frustration level is higher, and your job satisfaction is lower. Being a mom is hard enough. Why make life even harder by refusing to invest in what you need?

I'm certainly not suggesting you run out and purchase everything you need (or want) right now. Nor am I suggesting you spend money you don't have. I am suggesting you develop a method for determining what you need and find a way to finance it, even if it's just one piece of equipment or inventory. Focus on sustaining, improving, and growing your business (as long as doing so doesn't compromise your role of mother). Doing so will allow you to replace hesitancy with confidence and reluctance with wisdom as you seek to make wise equipment additions and to make your business as profitable as possible.

Lesson Learned: It takes money to make money. There's a difference between "spending" and "investing in your business." Smart CEOs look for wise investments and make them with confidence.

Work-at-Home Mom Profile

Joy Duling

Name and type of business:

A 25 Hour Day, LLC. A business strategy, coaching, and project support business.

How long have you been in business?

Three years.

Why did you choose this business?

I had been doing project management work in the government sector for seven years when my husband took a new job and we needed to relocate our family. While my management position offered a comfortable salary and benefits, I couldn't bear the idea of having to be on the road for two and a half hours a day, commuting. My initial business plan was framed around the idea of going "freelance." As I gained confidence in my ability to actually find paying work, I also realized that "just" being a contractor would never satisfy my overachiever tendencies. I needed to make a bigger splash. That's when I started to build more of a consulting practice infrastructure.

What's the toughest part of running a business and a family under one roof?

For me, the toughest part is dealing with other people's perceptions. Sometimes people think you're less serious about your business if you're home-based, and it can be hard to command desirable consulting fees. I've had prospects who have assumed that home-based means "no overhead." As a result, I try pretty hard not to look home-based. My marketing collateral is the highest quality I can possibly afford, and even though all of my real work is done from my home office, I also rent a small meeting space outside my home so that I have a separate physical address. For me, the little bit that I have to pay for rent each month has been well worth it, simply due to the increased fees that I'm able to charge. Today most people would never know I'm home-based. I like to think I've created a way to have the best of both worlds.

What unique child care strategies have you used to enable you to work successfully from home?

My daughter was nine when I started working from home, and she could entertain herself for extended periods of time. The only time child care became a serious issue was over summer break when a daily rant of "*Mom, I'm booooooooooored*" would drive me positively crazy. I do my best to patchwork together a summer schedule, juggling various day camps, Vacation Bible School, trips to stay with out-of-state grandparents, and so on. I also feel blessed to have a business that can be run from virtually anywhere. All I need is my laptop and my cell phone, and I can work on projects and connect with clients.

What's your favorite part of being in business for yourself?

For me, working from home while my daughter is in her middle school years has been absolutely priceless. This is a period of time during which she's becoming a young woman—her schoolwork's getting tougher, relationships more complicated, and peer influences more significant. I'm appreciative of the fact that I never have to worry about asking the "boss" if it's okay to take time off when my family needs me. My daughter also gets to see how I work on a daily basis. Not only does that create some unique mother-daughter moments, but she's also getting a firsthand, behind-the-scenes look at entrepreneurship. I hope that seeing the way I run my business provides my daughter with a different perspective on what is possible for her own life.

What's your least favorite part?

Having to assume complete responsibility for my own financial success or failure. I often say that my only financial goal for the first year was to keep the family from having to eat ramen noodles every meal, but the truth is that the financial part of self-employment can be really stressful. When I left my government job to be self-employed, my husband and I had agreed on a date by which my business *had* to be generating an income. If it wasn't, I needed to go back to work for someone else. Those were some of the most stressful months of my life. Even now, three years later, there are certainly days I miss having the comfort of a steady paycheck!

What do you know now that you wish you would have known when you started?

How much of what I would be doing would be marketing. I was at least six months into self-employment before I recognized that my primary job had to be "owning" the business. Shifting from the worker bee mentality to creating a sustainable business model that provides income and stability for my family is something I continue to work on.

What's the biggest mistake you've made as an at-home business owner?

Buying into the idea that I can do it "all" because I'm the one who is working from home has been a huge mistake. When I worked in a traditional workplace, my husband and I took turns on family obligations more. But once I started working from an in-home office, the lion's share of household responsibilities fell to me, and it became increasingly hard to justify "inconveniencing" my husband for things when I was already home or spending the money to hire housekeeping, laundry, meal preparation, or child care help.

What's the smartest move you've made as an at-home business owner?

Interestingly, while not delegating household chores is my biggest mistake, hiring help in my business was not an issue for me at all. I have one virtual assistant that I use as my primary assistant and then several others that I've called on for specific specialty projects including answering my phones and handling event registrations when I have a workshop planned or doing some project work when I've sunk into overwhelmed mode. Having good virtual assistants to call on gives me the capacity to do more in my business.

What's the most mortifying "mom moment" you've had in running your at-home business?

I think my most mortifying moment had to be about three years ago when we had just moved into the neighborhood and I had launched my business. I emerged one chilly October Saturday from my office cocoon and looked out the front window of my house to see my nine-year-old daughter strutting up and down the street, waving my good kitchen broom up to the sky and wearing the itty-bittiest tank top she could find, short shorts, and bright purple go-go boots. She insisted she looked just like Daphne from the Scooby-Doo cartoons and that the boots were enough to keep her plenty warm. All I could imagine was my brand-new neighbors shaking their heads and wondering where the poor child's mother could possibly be.

What advice would you give to another woman who is interested in starting her own work-at-home business?

A home-based business needs as much structure and planning and support as a traditional, out-of-home business, maybe even more. Without a "boss" to report to, it's very easy to slip into patterns of behavior that undermine your success. Be absolutely vigilant about protecting the time and space your business will need. Plan to spend at least as much time in marketing and business development as you do in delivering your product or service. If possible, join a business development or mastermind group that can keep you motivated and focused on the big picture.

Learn more about Joy's business at www.a25hourday.com.

17

subcontracting

surrounding yourself with a winning team

Early in my work-at-home career, I asked a successful real estate agent this question: "If you had one piece of advice to give someone who works for herself, what would it be?"

She was so certain of her answer, she didn't even pause to think. "Never do yourself what you can pay someone else to do," she responded.

I asked her to explain. "I'm a real estate agent," she said, "and the best use of my time is listing and selling houses. I hire someone to do everything else I need done." A graphic designer creates all her mailings for her, and a mailing house applies the postage and sorts the brochures according to postal regulations. An assistant sets up showings and confirms appointments. She focuses on securing listings, working with buyers, and selling properties. And that's how she has become successful.

I've taken her advice to heart, and so should you.

Obviously, when you're just starting out and money is tight, it makes sense to do as much as you can yourself. Eventually, however, you may experience the following and need to hire a subcontractor:

- You have too much work and not enough time to do it.
- A looming deadline makes it necessary to hire help.
- A project requires specialized skills you don't have.
- You choose to focus on what you're best at and subcontract all or a portion of the remainder of your work.

I currently work with several subcontractors on a regular basis. Two are graphic designers who create my marketing pieces and lay out the publications I edit, two are specialists who maintain my website, and one maintains my e-zine database, formats my newsletters each month, and sends them out for me. All are work-at-home moms. (I'd love to have you join me as a subscriber to my blog. Simply go to www.makingworkathomework.com and enter your email address in the registration box.)

By outsourcing these aspects of my business, I have:

- gained access to experts who help me promote my business professionally;
- freed up time in my schedule so I can focus on income-producing activities and meeting deadlines;
- saved myself the time and frustration it takes to learn how to do something new;
- expanded my reach and connected with readers conveniently and cost-effectively;
- grown my business without adding the overhead and head-aches that can be associated with employees.

After you've been in business for a time and have a little capital to work with, you may find it makes more "cents" (and dollars!) to focus on activities that produce income for your business and to outsource whatever else you can. Doing so is known as focusing on the "highest use of your time."

For a photographer, the "highest use of her time" is likely when she's behind the camera. It may also occur when she's meeting with potential clients to generate more business. Conversely, the "lowest use" of her time might be in front of a computer screen digitally enhancing her work. The "highest use" produces revenue or furthers her business. The "lowest use" does not, although it's still necessary.

> It may be wise for you to focus on activities that produce income for your business and to outsource whatever else you can.

Let's say the photographer we mentioned needs to move her portfolio online to help promote her business. Does it make more sense for her to do it herself or to hire someone to do it for her?

It depends. If she has the skills to develop a website, the interest in doing so, and the time available, it might make sense for her to design it. But if she lacks the skills and/or is pressed for time, it might actually make more sense to hire someone else to do the project.

When considering subcontracting, how do you know if it makes sense or not? There are actually two considerations. The first is financial.

Let's look at the example above. The photographer currently charges $75 per hour for her photography skills. She estimates it will take fifteen hours of her time to create a website. Designing the site herself would require forgoing $1,125 of income (15 hours x $75 per hour), assuming she could book all fifteen hours. By asking for referrals, however, she's found a web designer who charges $30 per hour for this type of work.

Because the designer is a skilled professional, she estimates it will only take her ten hours to complete the site. (Our photographer is already ahead by virtue of the fact that the professional can complete the project more quickly than she can.) In this case, the photographer can expect to pay $300 (10 hours x $30 per hour).

If she's able to book fifteen hours worth of work for herself during this time (the time it would have taken her to design her site), she'll earn $1,125. After she pays the web designer, she'll still have $825 in her pocket. In this case, it makes financial sense for the photographer to hire someone to design her website for her.

But what if the photographer only makes $30 an hour and the web designer charges $75 per hour? Or what if she's not able to book a photo shoot to cover the cost of hiring a designer? It still might make sense to hire someone else to do it. In addition to considering the financial aspect of hiring a subcontractor, the photographer should also ask:

- Do I have the skills to do the work?
- Am I interested in doing the work?
- Do I have the time to do the work?

If she has the skills, the interest, and the time, she may well decide to do the work herself even if she can afford to pay someone else to do it. If she doesn't have the skills, the interest, or the time, she'll need to find a way to pay for the work.

If she doesn't have adequate finances for the project, she may need to dip into the financial reserves she's set aside for such a situation (see chapter 20, "Rainy Days and Reinvesting"). Maybe she'll need to actively hunt for additional work so she can afford to hire someone. Or perhaps she can exchange her photography services for web design expertise. (However, she should check with her accountant first regarding the tax implications of bartering.)

Several years ago, when it became clear I needed an online presence, I took an HTML programming class. I wanted to know how difficult programming was, how long it took, and how much I really needed to know to build my own website. What I learned was this: I had no interest in learning web design whatsoever! In addition, the class taught me that web design was more than just programming.

An artist's eye (which I don't have) is necessary as well so that a site will be aesthetically pleasing in addition to being easy to navigate.

As a result of the class, I resolved to leave my web design needs to a professional. I have budgeted accordingly each year since.

Take a minute to think about the various jobs you do to sustain your business. Are there any you might be able to contract out? If so, the following guidelines will enable you to find the help you need and ensure that subcontracting helps your business instead of hindering it:

> Referrals are the best way to begin the process of searching for a subcontractor.

Ask for referrals. I never personally met the woman who created my early websites. She was referred by the woman who does my e-zine. They've never personally met either! (One lives in New York and the other in Utah.) How did we all find each other? By referral.

Referrals are the best way to begin the process of searching for a subcontractor. Ask friends, family, and other at-home CEOs who they've used or who they know who does the type of work you're looking for. (Referrals from people who have actually contracted with the referred individuals obviously should carry more weight than referrals from people who have only heard about the referred individuals.)

Shop around. Once you have a list of individuals, contact each one by phone or email to find out if they are accepting new business. If so, describe your project and ask if they would be interested in bidding on it. Cross off your list anyone who isn't able or interested in being considered.

Try to obtain bids from at least three contractors. This will give you an idea regarding the market value of the services and allow you to see how different contractors charge.

Be specific. The more you know about your project, the more accurate the bidding process will be. Telling a web designer you "need a website" isn't nearly as specific as telling a web designer you "need a ten-page website for which you'll write the copy and prepare a site map."

When determining the scope of your project, ask:

- Is this a one-time project or will it result in ongoing work for the contractor? (Contractors may be flexible in their initial fees if they know it may result in more work.)
- What exactly are you asking the subcontractor to do? If you need a marketing piece created, will the freelancer be writing *and* designing it or just designing it?
- Do you want the contractor to bid hourly, on the project as a whole, or both?
- What will you supply for the contractor (e.g., content, images, the domain name, and other materials)?
- How long will the contractor have to complete the work?

Ask questions. As you're talking to each contractor, ask for advice. Good questions to ask are:

- What's the most cost-effective way to do this?
- If we were to work together on this job, what would you require from me to be successful?
- How would you approach this project?
- How long do you think it will take for you to complete this job?

Asking questions of this nature does two things. First, it gives you an opportunity to learn more about each contractor's work style and approach—and to determine if he or she is compatible with how you prefer to work. Second, the process may provide you with insight and ideas you hadn't thought about prior to starting the project. The process of hiring subcontractors has often made my projects better because of the ideas I take away as the result of talking to a variety of professionals.

Arrange a phone or in-person meeting to discuss the bid. This will give you the opportunity to further assess the contractor's style. Is he easy to talk to? Does she answer your questions directly, thoroughly, and in a way you can easily understand? How well does he listen to you? Does this person seem like someone you could work with?

When my husband and I built our current home, we met with five builders personally before deciding which one to work with. We automatically took two out of consideration because their bids were so much higher than the others. We eliminated a third because during our meeting he refused to talk to or with me—instead preferring to communicate with my husband! Because my job was more flexible at the time, we knew I would be the primary contact for the builder. It was clear this guy wouldn't be comfortable with that, and neither would I. His demeanor during our meeting told us he wouldn't be a good match for us.

When you talk with a subcontractor by phone or in person, you'll pick up vibes that will be helpful as you consider who to hire for your project. Trust your instinct. I believe the relationship you have with your subcontractors is just as important, if not more, than their technical skill. It makes no sense to hire someone who's technically proficient if you aren't going to be able to communicate or work with her. It's essential to hire someone you trust and are comfortable with.

Don't buy on price alone. While you may be tempted to select the cheapest bid, this isn't always the wisest way to select a subcontractor. As mentioned above, there's more to subcontracting than cost. You want to be sure you're working with someone you trust and are comfortable with as well as someone who possesses the skills necessary to complete the job. After these criteria are met, then you should consider price.

You might decide to eliminate the highest bid you receive. Some individuals also eliminate the lowest bid, believing "you get what you pay for." While this is often true, my experience shows that many solo entrepreneurs (especially those who work at home) offer lower prices. Consequently, I personally don't automatically eliminate the lowest bid.

After eliminating some bids, compare the remaining ones along with what you know about the contractors who provided them. At this point, ask:

- Have you worked with any of these contractors before? If so, was the experience a good one?
- Which contractors came with the strongest referrals?
- If the price difference is negligible, which contractor do you feel most comfortable working with?
- Are you confident the contractor can complete the work in the given time frame?
- Which contractor are you most interested in working with? Or which one is your gut instinct telling you to hire?
- If the contractor you have identified is the most expensive, do you believe the quality of work you'll receive is worth the additional cost?

Once you've selected a subcontractor, be sure to seal your agreement in writing. The agreement doesn't have to be a fancy contract with lots of legalese, but it should outline what you're contracting for, when the project will be completed, who is responsible for what, and how the contractor will be compensated. For long projects, I find it's best to create a payment schedule. This could consist of 50 percent paid up front and 50 percent upon completion of the project. Or perhaps you'll pay the contractor monthly for a given number of months. You might set a ceiling, such as "$40 per hour, up to a total of $800." Most contractors have a payment policy that will dictate how you'll compensate them. If the policy isn't comfortable for you, don't hesitate to negotiate a plan that is. Be sure to sign this agreement and have the contractor you're working with do the same.

After you've worked successfully with a contractor, it may not be necessary to sign a letter of agreement for every project you do together, especially if the contractor is willing to bill you as work is completed and you have a clear understanding regarding the hourly rate.

Trust is involved when you work with subcontractors. As I mentioned, I never met the web designer who designed my earlier sites. At the beginning of our relationship, I was nervous about giving her access to my domain name passwords and hiring her to do such a large project without having worked with her previously. To allay my fears, we agreed we'd do the work in stages. First she'd create several designs for me to choose from. Once one was selected, she'd build a page using the designated design so I could see it implemented and approve it before the remainder of the site was created. By breaking this large job into smaller ones, both of us were protected. She did a little work at a time for my approval, and we were able to move through the project successfully.

When it was time to design a second site, I asked her to take the ball and run with it. She did so beautifully. Only one design was necessary because she's so clever and intuitive—skills I know I'm lacking—and she was able to implement the design in a way that was pleasing to the eye and also easy to navigate.

If I had chosen instead to buy the web design software that's now available, I'm sure I'd still be reading the directions and learning by trial and error. Instead, my site is online and I'm focused on one of the highest uses of my time: writing.

As well as following the guidelines I've just described, you'll want to be careful about a few things that might not have come to mind. Here are three cautions as you consider working with contractors:

For creative work, be sure to indicate who will own the rights to a project. Unless the project is identified as a "work for hire" in which all rights are transferred to you, it's possible that the contractor will own the rights. Rights and licensing are beyond the scope of this book, but you need to be aware of the implications. Be sure to discuss this with any contractors you hire to do creative work.

Beware of "getting a good deal." While it is possible to get a deal by having a friend's son design your website or provide other services you need, you should consider the intangible cost of the deal. If the son is a student, will he or she be able to finish the project in a timely manner? If you need someone to update the site, will he still be available—or away at college and unreachable? How much experience does he have? If he runs into difficulty, does he have the troubleshooting skills necessary to complete the project? Sometimes what costs little or nothing in terms of finances actually ends up being costly in terms of time, aggravation, and damage to a relationship.

Never do business with family or friends. An entrepreneurial cousin I admire once gave me this advice, and it seemed like a harsh policy when I heard it, especially since trust is such a large part of business. If you can't trust your friends and family, who can you trust?

It wasn't really trust my cousin was talking about, however. It was the fact that he places such high value on relationships with friends and family that he doesn't want to do anything to destroy them. A business disagreement, even the most minor one, can indeed be fatal to a relationship. My cousin was simply passing

162

along advice he'd learned the hard way, and it's advice I'm passing along to you.

If you do decide to do business with friends or family, be sure to discuss how you'll handle disagreements *before the business arrangement begins.* In addition, decide how you'll get out of the arrangement if it becomes clear that doing business together is damaging your bond. No business is worth damaging a relationship.

What's the highest use of *your* time? And what can you outsource? Though your business may not yet be mature enough to afford hiring subcontractors, doing so is a growth strategy you might consider in the future. By identifying now the highest use of your time as well as services you could outsource, you'll be in a better position to take advantage of subcontracting when it becomes necessary. And if you're currently drowning in your business and already know you could benefit by hiring help, now's the time to ask for referrals and to pick up the phone and begin asking for bids. Doing so is one way to help preserve both your profit and your sanity as a solopreneur.

Lesson Learned: Subcontracting is a smart way to find the skills you need to grow your business without the expense of employees.

18

boosting your revenue

lessons in working less and making more

If you've priced your goods and services appropriately, revenue leads to profit. If you are interested in increasing your profit, there are only five ways to do it:

1. Increase your revenue by selling more products or booking more business
2. Increase your fees or prices
3. Reduce your expenses
4. Develop new revenue streams
5. A combination of the above

For the past two years, my goal has been to work less and make more. It's not that I've gotten greedy. I just want to make sure I'm getting a fair return for my labor. And if I'm going to take time from my family, I want to make sure I'm adequately compensated.

Sometimes we underestimate our value as work-at-home moms because of lack of confidence or gratitude that we can work flexibly when others can't. A friend challenged my thinking in this regard when she flippantly said, "Just because you work in your pajamas sometimes doesn't mean your work is worth less than someone who gets dressed every day."

She's right. That's why we need to periodically take a look at our income and expense statement to ensure we're earning what we're worth and maximizing our profit. Here's how to measure your success in this regard:

Determine the minimum you have to work to cover your overhead. My profit was lean the first years of my home-based business because I was caring for a toddler and an infant and I wasn't able to do much else! Yet I still had overhead expenses such as a second phone line, Internet connection fee, and office supplies. Be sure your prices allow you to cover your overhead and make a profit. If you're a network marketer, be sure you're selling enough consistently so that your expenses are covered each month even if you're in a maintenance mode.

Identify the market value for your line of work. If you were employed by another company doing what you're doing, what would your salary be? Another way to think of this is to determine the "going rate" for your type of work—and then compare what you currently charge. Though you may be making somewhat less due to the fact you are not based in an office outside the home, may not be working full-time, and have flexibility that many employees don't have, your income should still be comparable. If it's not, it's time for an adjustment. A consultant I know increased her fees by 30 percent when she realized she was undercharging for her services. No one balked. If it's been a while since you've increased your rates, ask yourself if now's the time to do it again.

Examine your expenses. If your profit isn't what you want it to be, take a careful look at your expenses. Can you save by buying in bulk or shopping at a wholesale club? Use refurbished ink cartridges rather than buying new? Consolidate your phone and Internet with the same provider to reduce costs? Make do with the software you have rather than upgrading every time a new version comes out? Form a co-op with other work-at-home moms so you can buy in bulk and share the cost savings?

Actively looking for ways to reduce expenses is a challenging exercise and one that should be done at least annually. The lower your expenses, the higher your profit margin. But be sure you don't cut expenses to the point of compromising your effectiveness or causing you to have to work harder than you need to. Remember, it takes money to make money.

Be realistic. Though you may wish to sell more products or book more business, doing so will require you to work more than you are, unless you can find a way to handle the increase without additional effort. If you're a network marketer, you might choose to focus on building a bigger team underneath you. If you're an independent service professional, you might decide to market more aggressively but pass the increased workload along to subcontractors instead of handling it yourself.

As you set goals each year (which we'll discuss in the next chapter), be sure to recognize your limits in terms of time, energy, and capacity. If you choose to increase your income, be aware that doing so requires other increases as well, including the possibility of increased stress. If you don't want the anxiety that may accompany increasing your current sales levels, reduce your income expectations or increase your fees instead. Keep in mind there may be a point at which the market will no longer bear fee increases. If this is happening to you, consider developing new income streams for your business.

The more deliberate and intentional you are about focusing on your goals, the higher your likelihood of success.

If the idea of boosting your revenue seems complex, that's because it is. It's even trickier for work-at-home moms because our work time isn't always our own. Furthermore, in choosing to work alone, we limit our capacity.

If you're in the service business and you sell yourself instead of a product, you know there is only so much of you to go around. As much as I'd like to do more presentations each year, thereby increasing my income, doing so would require more travel and more nights away from home. That's why I've begun to look at developing new revenue streams such as conducting teleseminars, which allow me to use my training skills without leaving home. Though this isn't currently a large part of my business, it possibly could be.

You may or may not want to boost your revenue. I certainly didn't become serious about it until my children were out of elementary school. And I didn't really begin thinking about it until I realized that college is just a few short years away for my oldest.

When you're ready to focus on boosting your income, the tips above will be helpful. As with everything in life, the more deliberate and intentional you are about focusing on your goals, the higher your likelihood of success.

As you plan, remember that increases in revenue will require other increases as well. Be sure you're willing to make the necessary sacrifice or plan in such a way that you have a team to support your increases so you don't carry the burden alone. That's currently my focus. I'm asking, *How can I build a team around me so I can increase my revenue without actually doing all the work myself?* The answers are coming slowly. They are requiring me to change my thinking and also to ask where I want to be and what I want to be doing in five years. At this point, the future is fuzzy. But a vision is forming. And as it does, I get to decide how best to implement it. That's one of the great things about being an entrepreneur.

Walt Disney said, "If you can dream it, you can do it." As you're dreaming, dare to dream big.

Lesson Learned: Increasing revenue and profit requires increases in time, energy, capacity, and possibly stress. When you focus on boosting your revenue, be sure to consider the "cost" of these other increases as well.

Work-at-Home Mom Profile

Tammy Harrison

Name and type of business:
JDHarrison.com (web design and hosting) and Quiltalicious, LLC (quilt design).

How long have you been in business?
Since 1999.

Why did you choose this business?
I wanted to support my geeky side as a webmaster, but I also wanted to support my creative side in quilt design. Both businesses were chosen because I could do them from home . . . and my passion runs deep for working at home!

What's the toughest part of running a business and a family under one roof?
Respect for time—my time, my family's time, and my client's time. It's a fine balance to give everyone what they need.

What unique child care strategies have you used to enable you to work successfully from home?
None, really. My goal was to raise my children myself, and I've done that. We did send three of our children to preschool for one year just so they could have some social and structural experiences before starting kindergarten. Otherwise, I've been a mom most of the day, and I work late into the nights.

What's your favorite part of being in business for yourself?
Freedom to be me and to set my own schedule. Of course, what mom really gets to set her "own" schedule? I've appreciated having the freedom to allow my children to set my schedule! Honestly, it was probably more that I was raised by a mother who was at home all of the time. She died when I was twelve years old so I really wanted to make sure my children got as much of me as possible, just in case I wasn't long for this earth.

What's your least favorite part?
Probably having so much fun with my work that I have a hard time turning the computer off in the evenings.

What do you know now that you wish you would have known when you started?

The biggest lesson that I've learned is to ask for help when needed. That goes for all aspects of my life—to ask for help as a mom, as a wife, and as a business owner.

What's the biggest mistake you've made as an at-home business owner?

Getting involved in too many things.

What's the smartest move you've made as an at-home business owner?

Telling people "no" if what they wanted didn't meet my needs or interests.

What's the most mortifying "mom moment" you've had in running your at-home business?

I had sent my son to a Montessori preschool run by a member of the church we attended. He'd gone for half of a year in the mornings only, and it worked well. The next school year, I enrolled him for all day. On his first full day there, they did not change his pants a single time—even knowing he wasn't potty trained (it wasn't required). I'd let them know his supplies were in his bag when I dropped him off. When I took him to change his pants and put his jammies on (we'd not been home very long) and saw his red, welted bottom, I was *so* upset! Was I a bad mom? What could I have done differently? I took my children out of the school the next day and they never went back!

What advice would you give to another woman who is interested in starting her own work-at-home business?

You have to really be motivated to be successful working from home. You have to work twice as hard, in the beginning, to make sure you fulfill your personal needs and the needs of your family as well as move toward your goals with your business. Most of the women I have known who don't succeed are those who expected to be able to make a full-time income within a few short months of working from home. Unless you already have a successful business, this just doesn't happen. I've been working from home (not always full time) for twelve-plus years, and finally this year have made enough to support my family. It takes time, perseverance, and gumption to really make this lifestyle a success for all involved.

To learn more about Tammy's businesses, visit her websites at www.jdharrison.com and www.quiltalicious.com.

19

one-page planning

spend a morning, plan a year

What work-at-home mom has time for strategic planning?

It's a fair question. It's also the wrong question. Focusing on whether or not you have time to plan makes planning a scheduling issue when in reality it's a strategy issue.

Why plan? Planning allows you to:

- identify and focus on the "highest and best use of your time"
- develop a concrete plan for how you'll grow your business while growing your kids
- let go of mediocre and/or unprofitable ideas
- take an objective look at your business to identify strengths and weaknesses and to respond accordingly

I've been doing a one-page strategic plan for my business for the past six years. It's the single most important activity I do. I'll teach you how to do it in this chapter.

As a professional strategic planning facilitator, the biggest mistake I see organizations and individuals make is that they spend too much time planning and not enough time executing. They develop

> It's true in life and it's true in business: what we focus on expands.

lengthy plans that are too complex to be relevant or helpful on a daily basis. That's why I appreciate the value of a one-page plan. Mine is posted on the wall in my office so I can refer to it whenever necessary. It consists of 111 words.

These 111 words help narrow my focus each year. And here's an important truth: *what we focus on expands.*

It's true in life and it's true in business. If we focus on lack of sales, we become discouraged. If we focus on developing new sources of sales, we get energized.

If we focus on the fact that our kids bother us and make it difficult to work, we'll forget to be thankful that we have them.

If we focus on how hard it is to run a business and a family under one roof, we'll no longer notice or appreciate the benefits of doing so.

What you focus on expands. That's why a one-page plan is so important.

For most of us, just getting through each day successfully takes all we have. Consequently, we don't have much left over for new ideas and initiatives or to focus on how we could be running our business more effectively. We're just focused on running the business, period.

The value of a one-page map is that we set aside some time to look at what's working—and what's not—and to plan accordingly. My planning day is a gift to myself as an entrepreneur. It helps settle me, focuses me, and gives me the time and space I need to take an unhurried, objective look at where I've been and where I'm going. Sometimes it's the only day of the year that I really have the opportunity to do that.

Before we move to the nitty-gritty of planning, let me make a few suggestions. First, don't look at this as another thing on your to-do list. If you do, it will feel more like a chore than the freeing exercise it is.

In addition, make your planning time special so that you look forward to it rather than dread it. I personally take a half day in December for this purpose. I mark a day off on my calendar and am careful to protect the time for its intended purpose. By choosing a day in December, I guarantee I'll have at least one day of rest in a month that's otherwise rushed and full. Since it's the end of the year, it's a good time to look ahead. Planning can occur at any time, however, and if you're willing to try it, don't feel it's necessary to wait until the end of the year. There's nothing magical about when you do it. The magic happens simply because you take the time to do it and because you reap immense rewards.

Setting the Stage

There is no one "right way" to develop a plan. I'm sharing how I do it in the hope that it will give you some ideas and help you adapt the process so that it works for you.

If you have young children, planning to plan is necessary so you'll be able to arrange for child care. I did my first plan when my son was preschool age. I traded babysitting with a friend to secure the solitude I needed. If you have young children, it's best to do your planning when they are asleep or not around.

When your planning time arrives, treat yourself. I like to head to my favorite room in the house, light a candle, and begin working. Other people have told me they like to listen to upbeat music or take their legal pad or laptop to a coffee shop where they can draw energy from the vibes around them. I begin by handwriting my thoughts because the process of transitioning them from my head to my hand to paper helps me clarify my thinking. Others wouldn't dream of doing this when they can simply begin typing on the computer, developing a final document as they work. Do whatever is best for you.

Regardless of the environment you choose, be sure you are comfortable. This will enable you to do your best work. (I find working in my pajamas is most effective for me, which is why I haven't yet ventured to a coffee shop to develop my plan. Maybe next year!)

> Your greatest potential for growth comes from capitalizing on your strengths, not focusing on your weaknesses.

The last thing required to set the stage is to approach the exercise with honesty. This may require you to admit things are not working perfectly, or you're not handling the work-family balance as well as you'd like, or you're not happy doing what you're doing. All of this is valuable information. You can't solve a problem without first understanding what it is.

An honest approach to planning also requires you to examine what *is* working well, to identify what you'd like to be more focused on, to acknowledge what you're grateful for, and to focus on the strengths you bring to the business. Sometimes this is just as hard as looking at what's not working because it requires us to acknowledge our unique abilities. Many of us were told as children to "be humble" and "not to brag," making it difficult for us to be able to complete the self-scrutiny required for strategic planning. The sooner you move past any inability to recognize and capitalize on your own strengths, the better off both you and your business will be. In fact, *your greatest potential for growth comes from capitalizing on your strengths, not focusing on your weaknesses.* This is a lesson I've learned only recently. Because of it, I'm now asking myself, "How can I be more of who I naturally am?" The question may be helpful to you, too. In addition, you'll want to ask:

- What areas of your business are running smoothly?
- What areas aren't running smoothly?
- What areas are most challenging for you?
- What obstacles do you face in running your business?
- What are your favorite responsibilities in running your business and how could you focus more on these?
- What are your least favorite responsibilities in running your business and is there a way to outsource these?
- Is there something you should be asking yourself that you haven't asked yet?
- What is the one thing that would make the most difference for your business over the next year if you were to do it?

As you consider the above, handwrite or type your answers. Don't stop to censor what you're writing. Simply focus on getting your thoughts down on paper. It's essential to empty your brain of everything that's floating around before you proceed to the next step.

If you're like me, your mind will wander a bit while you're working on your plan. I keep a small notepad next to me so that when I think of things I need to do, I can jot them down and keep working without being afraid of forgetting something. Inevitably, during this exercise I'll remember I need to send a card to someone, RSVP to a child's birthday party, buy socks for my son, or all of the above. The notepad makes it possible for me to capture this list of chores without seriously interrupting my planning process.

What's Next?

After you've emptied your mind on paper, you'll likely be able to see some common themes or identify ideas that make the most sense for you to pursue over the upcoming year. As you work to narrow your focus, it may help to use a highlighting marker to divide your thoughts into two categories: most relevant and important and least relevant and important.

As you study your list, your goal should be to identify three to five areas of focus over the upcoming year. I usually choose five, with the knowledge that by the end of the year I will likely have accomplished only four. I find that usually something I thought I wanted to do ends up on the list only because I thought it should be there. When I recognize this goal for what it is (a "should" instead of a "want to"), I give myself permission to drop it. This helps me further narrow my list and focus on what I have the energy, desire, and interest to accomplish.

Remember there is no right way to construct a plan. You can follow my suggestions or adapt them in a way that works for you. Certainly my way of doing this isn't the only way. And it may not even be the best way, but it works, which is valuable in and of itself.

After narrowing the list of possibilities, I write them out individually, starting with an action word such as "develop" or "register" or "learn." I list them separately on my final document but don't rank them in order of importance because I think all of them are important for different reasons. (If ranking your list will help you be more effective, then by all means, do it!)

After my planning is complete, I head to my computer, open a document, and type in bold "(Year) Goals and Objectives" at the top. After that I include Proverbs 16:9, which says, "In his heart a man plans his course, but the LORD determines his steps." This reminds me that despite my best laid plans, much is out of my control. My job is simply to do the best I can.

Some years I've created a vision for myself, while other years I've gone without. If you choose to use a vision, it should appear at the top of your document before you list your goals. When you're done, your plan might look like this:

ONE-PAGE BUSINESS PLAN

Vision

To help promote self-esteem and self-confidence in women and men who use my products and to use the proceeds of my business to bless my family and help others.

MY FOCUS FOR (Year)

1. Add at least five new individuals to my network.
2. Organize, computerize, and systematize my business so that I am more efficient, including learning to use database management software.
3. Increase my net profit by 15 percent this year.
4. Determine what I can hire someone else to do and hire an individual to do these things.
5. Set up an online store to help increase profits and allow customers to order at their convenience.

Your plan will be as unique as you are. When done properly, it will reflect your circumstances, the stage of your business, your season of mothering, and your desired growth goals for your business. When I began this process, I also included a gross income figure. I stopped doing this when my financial goal overtook my commitment to my family. However, if you thrive on meeting goals or need additional incentive this year, you might consider setting a monetary goal for yourself.

Implementing Your Plan

The purpose of planning is to help you gain clarity and focus, not to create stress. In fact, if reading this chapter makes you feel stressed, feel free to skip the remainder. You can come back later if you'd like or forego it altogether. Whatever you decide, remember it's best to put your own personal touches on the planning process so that it's most helpful and meaningful to you.

Since you'll be living with your plan for a full year, I suggest sleeping on it before you finalize it. Once you do, post the plan in a prominent location and refer to it often. As I mentioned, mine is on the wall of my office so I can easily reference it when making scheduling decisions and setting priorities.

For this process to be as effective as possible for you, it's necessary to review your plan periodically. You might even jot a reminder on your calendar for this purpose. As you review it, you may need to make revisions due to changes in circumstances, health, and so on. I consider my plan a "living document," which means I'm willing to change it as I gain new information.

Even if you don't go through the formal process of preparing a written plan, asking yourself the questions in this chapter is beneficial since doing so will help narrow your focus for the upcoming year.

If the process of developing a plan seems like a lot of work, don't be fooled. I am amazed how I can spend just a few hours and gain enough focus to positively influence my business. The return on investment is enormous. In fact, I credit it for the longevity of my business.

If you're still not convinced, read what Leslie Charles has to say about planning:

> In 1997, instead of drafting a long list of New Year's resolutions as I had in the past, I dedicated that entire year to one behavior: patience. Well, they say be careful what you ask for. 1997 brought me a bumper crop of tediously long lines, traffic tie-ups, brain-numbingly sluggish consumer transactions, delayed or canceled flights, long, slow trains, and other inconveniences.
>
> But every time I began feeling cranky or impatient, I remembered my "patience project" and forced myself to smile, relax, and let go, in spite of it all. Here's what I learned: Most of us are not persistent enough when it comes to change. We give up way too soon. But having a whole year to focus on one single behavior tips the scale in your favor. For once, time is on your side.[1]

The same is true with one-page planning. Focusing on five specific goals, instead of being overwhelmed with all you could or should be doing, tips the scale in your favor. Time is on your side when you focus on one or three or five things that will make the biggest difference over the next year if you do them. A one-page plan helps you identify them. Once you do, you can get to work. It's a powerful process.

Lesson Learned: What we focus on expands. Developing a one-page strategic plan is a powerful way to set goals and determine what your business requires for the upcoming year.

20

rainy days and reinvesting

creating peace of mind from your profit

If self-employment were easy, more individuals would take the plunge. Though it can be wonderfully freeing and flexible, it also comes with its share of headaches, including irregular income. It's certainly not like working for someone where you receive a paycheck every two weeks. Some weeks I deposit multiple checks and some months only one or two. That's where a rainy day fund comes in handy.

Financial experts recommend an emergency fund of three to eight times your monthly expenses. It may sound like an impossible goal, but if you take baby steps, eventually you'll get there. You should do this not only for your family finances but for your business as well. That way a lean month won't discourage you or cause undue stress. Plus, a contingency fund will enable you to have the flexibility to meet unexpected needs, such as extended illness or a child's special challenges. If you don't have a rainy day fund for your business, now's the time to start one. Here's how:

Set a goal. Look back over your business expenses for the past year or two, depending on how long you've been in business. (If you're just starting, use your best judgment. Then reevaluate your needs in six months when you have more financial data to work with.) Add your total expenses and then divide by the number of months over which they were incurred. This will give you your average monthly expense. (For example, if your expenses last year were $24,000, dividing by 12 will give you an average expense of $2,000 per month.) Multiply this number by three to determine the minimum savings you should accumulate in your contingency fund.

Though three months is the minimum recommended by financial experts, some suggest earmarking up to eight months' worth of expenses. Determine what's most comfortable for you. Some individuals feel exposed with just a few months' coverage while others feel that six or eight months' worth is too much. Take a look at your situation, including the stability of other family income, to determine what's best for you.

If you have large fluctuations in your monthly income (as in direct sales) or your work is seasonal (as in tutoring), it makes sense to have more in your emergency fund than if your income is more steady. As you analyze your business data, consider your family's overall financial situation as well. The weaker it is, the more you may want to put away in your emergency fund.

Open a separate account. To truly be an emergency fund, money should be set aside in a separate account. This way you will face less temptation to dip into the fund in nonemergency situations. Plus, you can invest this money and enjoy a return that will help the fund grow.

Develop a surefire savings plan. Determine how much you can reasonably put away each month—then figure out a way to make it happen. Will you deposit a percentage of your income into the contingency fund each time you receive payment for goods or services?

Will you establish an automatic transfer from your business checking account to your savings account until you reach your goal? Having a target is worthless if you don't also have a plan to reach it.

Reevaluate yearly. As your business grows, your income and expenses will likely grow too. What may have been sufficient in the first years of your business may no longer be enough to meet your needs if disaster were to strike. As you review your tax form each year (you're likely filing a Schedule C if you're not incorporated), note your expenses and then determine if you have enough savings to cover several months' worth if necessary. If not, boost your savings until you do.

Refresh quickly. If you need to dip into your rainy day fund, be sure to replenish it as soon as you are able. Depleting the fund leaves you vulnerable for the future, and you defeat the purpose of having one to begin with if you don't maintain adequate resources.

Money in the bank equals peace of mind. If you're living paycheck to paycheck, it may be hard to figure out a way to create a rainy day fund. It may take you a long time to save even a few months' worth of expenses. But every journey starts with a single step. If you don't start saving now, you'll never have a contingency fund.

As you start the saving process, it may be helpful to remember this: you won't miss money you don't see. In other words, if you can arrange for direct deposit into your savings account or automatically make the deposit yourself whenever you cash a check (even if the deposit is for a small amount), you won't miss the money. Begin the habit of paying yourself first, and soon you'll have both a rainy day fund and the peace of mind that comes with it.

Reinvestment

"Real" businesses don't skimp on investing in the future. And since you're serious about your enterprise, you shouldn't either.

Sometimes it's difficult to make a large business expenditure when you know you also have to buy school supplies or jeans or new shoes for the kids. As moms, we often find it hard to mentally separate our personal finances from our business finances. But it's necessary in order to make the kinds of investments we need to make in our companies, as discussed previously in the chapter on purchasing equipment.

Since the beginning of my entrepreneurial life, I've earmarked a portion of my income for reinvestment into the business. When I needed a new laptop two years ago, I had the money. When I needed to buy new inventory for my resource table, I had the money. When it was time to revamp my website, I had the money.

"Real" businesses don't skimp on investing in the future. And since you're serious about your enterprise, you shouldn't either.

This doesn't mean I spend wildly or willfully. I'm very deliberate and thoughtful regarding expenditures. I spend time determining if things are "needs" or "wants." But I've also (finally!) realized that trying to save money sometimes hurts my prospects in the long run and makes running an at-home enterprise even more difficult than it needs to be.

I have a question I ask myself when it comes to reinvestments or large expenditures: *if I were an employee and worked for someone else, would I recommend this expenditure to my boss to move the business forward?* If the answer is yes, I know the decision warrants consideration.

Obviously, investment in the future is much easier when you have the funds available. I feel better spending if I don't have to borrow or scrimp to get what I need. That's why I continually set aside money for both rainy days and reinvestment. It may not always be possible to fund future needs with current funds, however, and sometimes it is necessary to take out a loan or seek other financing. That's okay. Remember, if you worked for someone else and would recommend they do it to move the business forward, you should be willing to consider it as well. That's how businesses, at-home or not, develop fully. As you're helping your business realize its full potential, there's a good chance you'll be realizing yours as well.

Lesson Learned: Savings lead to peace of mind and the ability to reinvest in your business when necessary.

Work-at-Home Mom Profile

Jennifer Swanson

Name and type of business:

Jennifer Swanson, LLC, teaches people practical ways to simplify their lives. Services include private consulting (professional organizing in person and remotely via phone or email); public speaking (seminars, audio programs, and radio interviews); and writing (in print and online, plus free monthly e-newsletters).

How long have you been in business?

Five years.

Why did you choose this business?

A five-week stint of pregnancy bed rest really started it all, and it turned out to be a blessing in disguise. I developed a passion for simplicity and wanted to share it with others who wanted less clutter and more peace in their homes, offices, and schedules. I had always wanted a business with hours I could regulate according to my family's ever-changing seasons. This type of business also requires very little space in my home.

What's the toughest part of running a business and a family under one roof?

Holding back creative projects for my business. With more ideas than I can implement, it's easy to get distracted and make my family wait.

What unique child care strategies have you used to enable you to work successfully from home?

1. Scheduling early-morning phone consultations with long-distance clients who also have children at home
2. Scheduling evening and weekend seminars when Daddy's home
3. Advertising my consulting services in areas near Grandma's house
4. Networking with homeschooling families
5. Using babysitters during summers and school breaks
6. Maximizing the child care at the health club
7. Working late at night when my husband travels

What's your favorite part of being in business for yourself?

I love being an entrepreneur: the variety, the flexibility, and the stimulation. I've been able to foster opportunities that I would never have been able to pull off otherwise. I've made connections with extraordinary people all over the world. And, of course, I've enjoyed the tax benefits.

What's your least favorite part?

Fighting the labels. You're not a full-time at-home mom or a full-time career woman. Both camps ask a lot of questions about how I "do it all," which I don't.

What do you know now that you wish you would have known when you started?

The spiritual discipline of reflection and journaling. What brought you joy today? What made you upset? Where is God in all this? It helps uncover patterns and purpose within all aspects of life. Looking back helps you see more clearly what's working and what isn't so you can make more progress looking forward.

What's the biggest mistake you've made as an at-home business owner?

Paying hundreds of dollars for a boost-your-business-type program that didn't tell me anything I didn't already know or wasn't already doing. I made faster progress with one-on-one coaching from experienced professionals in my field.

What's the smartest move you've made as an at-home business owner?

Naming my company after myself. It gives uniqueness to my brand, makes me easy to find on the Internet, and allows my business to evolve in many directions.

What's the most mortifying "mom moment" you've had in running your at-home business?

As a favor to a friend, I gave a seminar to a group with child care on-site. Halfway through my talk, I turned around to see a woman holding my two-year-old son. That's when I learned about their "no diaper change" policy. That was the first and last time I took my children with me.

What advice would you give to another woman who is interested in starting her own work-at-home business?

It's important to get organized. If you can find what you need when you need it, you can spend more time making money and less time looking for things.

Hold your children tightly and your business loosely. Don't let perfectionism slow you down. And don't check your email so much.

Learn more about Jennifer at www.JenniferSwanson.com.

21

retirement planning

feathering your own nest

I know. How in the world can you begin to think about retirement while you're still changing diapers, wiping noses, and driving kids around?

It may be difficult, but the sooner you start, the better off you'll be. And when you plan carefully, you can actually reduce your tax burden while simultaneously investing in your future.

You've read that the reason I work is to earn money for groceries, orthodontics, and college tuition. I also work to fund our retirement. Each year I make sure to max out what I can put away toward building a retirement nest egg. I know I'm lucky to be able to do it. But it's also a matter of priorities. I'd rather put a chunk of change away for the future than drive a new car today. The result is that I've been able to put away the maximum allowed each year that I've been self-employed. Though the fund is growing slowly, it's growing. Better yet, instead of sending an even larger check to the IRS each year, I'm keeping more of my income for myself.

Please do not stop reading at this point, even if you're feeling intimidated or that there's no way you could possibly save for retirement. It's important you see the possibilities for yourself and *save whatever you can, even if it's just a few hundred dollars a year.* Why? Because it's possible to reduce your tax burden *and* save for retirement at the same time. It's one of the very few benefits of being self-employed. In my mind, it's a *must do* for at-home workers, even if your current budget is strained and money is an issue for you.

> When you plan carefully, you can actually reduce your tax burden while simultaneously investing in your future.

Any contribution you make to a designated retirement account (such as a SEP-IRA) will reduce your tax burden while increasing your retirement savings.

For example, let's say your household income is $50,000, of which $20,000 is from your business. (These are even numbers to make it easy to show you the math.) The government allows you to deduct your self-employed retirement contribution from your gross household income to determine the adjusted gross income you'll be taxed on. This is one area in which self-employed individuals have a bit of an advantage.

Here's how it works:

Net income from your business	$20,000
Minus maximum allowable SEP contribution	($3,717)
Adjusted income	$16,283

Obviously, the more net income you have, the higher your contribution will be. (To determine your maximum contribution, type "self-employed retirement calculator" into your favorite online search engine. Or go to http://finance.yahoo.com/calculator/ career-work/qua-12, which is the calculator I used for our example.) Maximums differ based on the plan you choose, which we'll discuss in a minute.

A little sacrifice today can provide for tomorrow.

In this scenario, you've reduced your taxable income by $3,717 and put that money in your retirement account. If you're in a 15 percent tax bracket, you've avoided paying an additional $558 ($3,717 x 15 percent) in taxes and saved $3,717 toward your future!

At this point you may be thinking, *There's no way we can afford to put that kind of money in a retirement account. We're struggling as it is.*

Let me challenge you. If you're not comfortable putting away the full amount you're permitted, would you consider stretching and saving 25 percent of the maximum allowed? If that still feels like too much, could you save 10 percent of the maximum?

Regardless of what you actually put in, it's foolish not to take advantage of this self-employed tax benefit. Here's why:

> Let's say you save $2,000 every year for 20 years, and your invest-
> ments earn 8 percent annually. If you start at age 25 and contribute
> until age 45 and then save nothing further, by age 65 you'd have
> roughly $426,000. But if you wait until age 35 to begin saving $2,000
> a year for 20 years and then retire at 65, your kitty would amount
> to about $198,000. In both scenarios your out-of-pocket contribu-
> tion is $40,000.[1]

When I talk to at-home entrepreneurs, eyes begin glazing over when I use the words *taxes* and *retirement*. I understand because neither used to interest me either. But stretching yourself now takes advantage of the value of compounding, which can quickly accelerate the value of your savings. Now that I've seen what a little sacrifice today can provide for tomorrow, I'm very interested in learning how to pay less in taxes and keep more for the future. As a smart entrepreneur, you should be too.

I know what you're thinking because I've heard these objections many times before. Is yours on the following list?

- We can't afford to save right now.
- I don't want to put money away where I can't reach it if I need it.
- I don't understand taxes.
- I don't want to understand taxes.
- I have no idea what a SEP-IRA is and no idea where to go to establish one.
- We have too much debt to even begin to think about saving.
- My husband does our taxes. I just sign the form each year.

Maybe you have an objection I haven't heard before. If so, feel free to add it to the list. Then splash some cold water on your face—it's time for a reality check!

If you're not saving for retirement, you're not going to be able to retire. Period.

Analysts predict the Social Security system may well be bankrupt before you and I receive our share. And it's predicted that without reform, the Medicare trust fund will become insolvent in the year 2019.[2]

I don't mean to be depressing, but too many people have their heads stuck in the sand when it comes to saving today so they have something in the bank tomorrow. Please don't be one of those individuals. With careful planning now and a willingness to sacrifice some, you can have the retirement you hope for. In addition, consider what author Cynthia Sumner says about retirement planning:

> While putting aside funds for your child's college education is important, it's more crucial to prepare for your own future. Your child will likely have access to other resources like scholarships, student loans, and part-time jobs, while . . . you may not. Even if kids have to rely on other sources of income during their college years, most would probably find that preferable to supporting you later when they have kids of their own to worry about.[3]

Your work at home gives you the opportunity to save for retirement in ways other individuals don't have. Generally, self-employed individuals select from four self-employed retirement plans:

- SEP-IRA
- SIMPLE IRA
- Individual 401(k)
- Defined benefit plan

Though I'm not a tax adviser, here's a brief overview of each option to start you thinking about this topic. (It may be easier for you *not* to think about it, but it's certainly not wiser.) I've listed options from the simplest to the most complex.

SEP-IRA

SEP stands for Simplified Employer Pension plan, and it really is simple. A SEP allows you to contribute up to 25 percent of your compensation (up to a maximum of $46,000 for 2008). Contributions are tax deductible and investment earnings grow tax deferred. Withdrawals after age 59 1/2 are taxed as ordinary income. Contributions are completely discretionary and can vary from year to year depending on your profitability and individual circumstances. SEP-IRA accounts are easy to set up and maintain, inexpensive, and don't require annual IRS filings. A SEP must be established and funded by your tax filing deadline.

SIMPLE IRA

A SIMPLE (Savings Incentive Match Plan for Employees) IRA is available to small businesses with less than 100 employees (including sole proprietorships) and includes two parts: an optional employee salary deferral, like a 401(k) plan, and a mandatory employer match. Employees (that's you!) can elect to defer up to 100 percent of their income up to a maximum of $10,500 (in 2008). Contributions are tax deductible and investment earnings grow tax deferred. Withdrawals after age 59 1/2 are taxed as ordinary income. Simple IRAs are easy to administer, inexpensive to maintain, and don't require IRS filings. They must be established by October 1 to be eligible for contribution for the current year.

The main difference between a SIMPLE IRA and a SEP-IRA is the mandatory employer match on behalf of eligible employees and in your own account. Unlike a SEP account, a contribution must be made each year and an employer match is mandatory. This may be okay if you're the only employee, but if you ever plan to hire employees, you should take this into consideration.

Individual 401(k)

An Individual 401(k) allows for greater contributions than SEP or SIMPLE IRAs, thereby maximizing contributions and valuable tax deductions. It allows you the flexibility to borrow against the value of your plan. Contributions can be as high as $46,000 a year (for 2008) based on a preset formula. Contributions are tax deductible and investment earnings grow tax deferred. Withdrawals after age 59 1/2 are taxed as ordinary income. Contributions are completely discretionary and can vary from year to year depending on your profitability and individual circumstances. Compared to a traditional 401(k), the individual plan is easy to maintain because administration is minimal. However, fees vary based on the plan administrator.

The deadline for establishing an Individual 401(k) is December 31 of the year in which you would like to receive the tax deduction. The deadline for depositing salary deferrals into the Individual 401(k) is generally your personal tax filing deadline.

Defined Benefit Plans

This is the most complicated and expensive type of self-employed retirement plan, but it allows for substantial tax deductible retirement contributions and significant future retirement income. A defined benefit plan allows contributions designed to fund a chosen level of retirement income at a predetermined retirement date. Contributions are determined by an actuarial formula. These plans are especially useful for older individuals and/or those who have a high earned income. Because these plans are more complex, it makes sense to work with a plan administrator to set one up.

Contribution Comparisons

Because different plans have different contribution maximums, you'll want to carefully consider your goals before choosing a plan. Based on our earlier example of $20,000 net income, here's how the maximum allowable amounts stack up for the three simplest plans:[4]

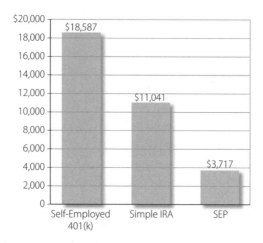

192

As you can see, a self-employed 401(k) offers the greatest savings opportunity, but remember that the cost of administering the plan is also likely the highest among these three options. And while a SIMPLE IRA offers a higher maximum in our example than a SEP-IRA, it requires a mandatory contribution for employees, something you may or may not be interested in. Though offering the lowest maximum savings in our example, a SEP-IRA is inexpensive, easy to set up, and doesn't require a mandatory contribution each year, offering flexibility that's attractive to many work-at-home moms.

Though the above are the most common self-employment retirement plans, you might also consider a traditional IRA, which will allow you to contribute up to $5,000 per year ($6,000 if you are 50 or older) beginning in 2008. The contribution is deductible if you are not covered by another plan. However, qualified distributions are taxed as ordinary income.

Another possibility is a Roth IRA. Though contributions are not deductible and therefore not as attractive to self-employeds, qualified distributions are tax free. The contribution limits in 2008 are the same as those listed above for the traditional IRA.

As you can see, there are plenty of retirement savings options for self-employed individuals. Because of varying rules, it's sometimes difficult to make comparisons between plans to understand which is best for you. That's where an accountant and financial planner are helpful.

If you're interested in starting a retirement account, follow these steps:

If you are married, make sure your husband is on board. Retirement planning is long-term, and putting away money for tomorrow often requires sacrifice today. Be sure your husband supports what you plan to do. If he's covered by a retirement plan, don't be content to let him be the only one to save. You'll miss tax-reducing benefits if you do.

Meet with a retirement planner. Most planners will meet with you on a complimentary basis to help you determine which option is right for you. In addition to enabling you to make a wise retirement decision, this meeting will also give you the opportunity to determine if you're comfortable with this individual. If so, consider setting up your plan with him or her.

If your husband has questions about self-employed retirement accounts, invite him to attend this meeting with you. That way you'll have a professional to help you handle your husband's questions or concerns.

Set aside money throughout the year so you're able to fund your plan without difficulty. Because maximizing my retirement contribution is a priority for me, I watch my checking account balance to make sure I'll have sufficient funds to contribute to my SEP-IRA each year. It's tough to do sometimes because I'm often making estimated tax payments near the contribution deadline. It's easier to maximize my retirement plan contribution when I plan carefully rather than simply hoping for the best each year.

> Plan carefully rather than simply hoping for the best each year.

Be flexible. If you choose a plan that doesn't require a mandatory contribution each year, you'll have the flexibility necessary to forego making a contribution if circumstances make it difficult to do so. A spouse's unemployment, an unexpected drop in your self-employed income, or family illness may make it difficult for you to fully fund your retirement every year. Many women I interviewed shared how their business is in "maintenance mode" due to child care responsibilities. This is where a flexible plan comes in handy. Allow yourself to take a pass when circumstances warrant, but if you're serious about saving for retirement, make sure this doesn't become the norm. And if you're not able to fully fund your retirement for the year, consider making a lower contribution that works with your current circumstances. Remember, something is always better than nothing when it comes to saving for retirement.

If you're not currently taking advantage of the fact that you can lower your adjusted gross income by saving for retirement, this might be the wisest decision you can make as an at-home CEO this year. It's certainly one you'll never regret—but one you may well regret *not* making.

Lesson Learned: Not only do smart at-home entrepreneurs actively plan their working life, they also plan for their post-work life.

Work-at-Home Mom Profile

Patti Chadwick

Name and type of business:

PC Publications. The business encompasses online bookselling, print publishing, e-publishing, website management, freelance writing, and public speaking.

How long have you been in business?

I began PC Publications in 1999.

Why did you choose this business?

I didn't really choose this business; it evolved. I have a passion for all things in print. I have been a bookseller for fifteen years. When I was introduced to the Internet, I was enthralled with all the information and decided I wanted to be a part of that. I began by building a website for selling books and then started an online magazine called *History's Women* (www.historyswomen.com). I published many articles on the website and then a book on the topic (which I self-published because I wanted to retain all the rights). I began selling the book on the website, which went well.

People started contacting me to sell their books (especially self-published authors). I self-published more books and helped others self-publish theirs and then sold them on my site.

Over the years, I learned the basics of building a website and managing an email list. I began sending out email newsletters for my websites and managing my sites. I took on volunteer projects to help nonprofits create e-newsletters and manage their lists. This led to meeting several authors who were willing to pay me to create and send their e-newsletters and manage their lists. This has become a very important part of my business.

I also sell used books on Amazon.com. I began this branch of the business with my youngest son. I go book scouting, buy the books, and take care of the paperwork. He puts them on Amazon and fulfills the orders. It's worked out well.

What's the toughest part of running a business and a family under one roof?

Closing down the office and leaving the work behind. Especially at the beginning. I found myself working night and day and missing time with my kids because it was hard to stop working because it was always "there." I did learn how to separate my personal life and business life most of the time, but it does overlap.

What unique child care strategies have you used to enable you to work successfully from home?

My kids were older when I began PC Publications, so I didn't have to do too much finagling with child care. As a precursor to PC Publications, I used to sell Usborne books at home parties when I homeschooled my children (and they were much younger). I made my children part of the business, and they helped me at the parties and by filling the orders. They earned some cash, and I didn't have to hire a babysitter!

What's your favorite part of being in business for yourself?

The freedom to work when I want and to work at *what* I want. It allows me to pursue my passions. Don't get me wrong; it is hard work, and I do have tasks I don't particularly enjoy, but I call the shots and form my schedule. If I can't work on Monday during the day, I can work at night and still meet my deadline. If I need a week off, I can tell my clients I'm off that week and make arrangements with them to complete their work. I can put my Amazon store on "vacation" if I want to take off. I can be there for sick kids (even if they are nineteen) and for my aging parents. I can volunteer at human service agencies and my church and not have to fit them around a regular nine-to-five job.

What's your least favorite part?

Not having a set weekly paycheck. But in today's economy, that isn't a sure thing anymore anyway!

What do you know now that you wish you would have known when you started?

I wish I had known more about website management and marketing online.

What's the biggest mistake you've made as an at-home business owner?

Letting the business consume my life at the beginning. I remember when my daughter was sick and I was busy meeting a deadline. She was a young teen, but she doesn't "do sick" well. She was in her room, and I gave her my cell phone and told her to call me if she needed me. While she was upstairs "practically dying," I was downstairs on the computer. She finally called me and said "*Mommmm* . . . I could be dead and no one would know!" It hit me then that the business I started to have the freedom to be with my kids was actually keeping me from them when they needed me. I knew that had to change, and it did.

What's the smartest move you've made as an at-home business owner?
Hired a good accountant and excellent tech support.

What's the most mortifying "mom moment" you've had in running your at-home business?
Being taped by the local news and having my son say I worked in my pajamas.

What advice would you give to another woman who is interested in starting her own work-at-home business?
Find your passion and pursue it. The best advice I received was "do what you love and the money will come." I pass that on to you. It may be slow, but you will succeed. And it doesn't seem like work when you love to do it!

It's amazing to look back and see how it all began by my selling books at home parties and writing for my church newsletter. It has evolved into a multifaceted business that helps me support my family with the freedom to tend to the home fires when needed. I work hard, but I can fit the business around my schedule and can work from anywhere in the world! There are many branches to my business, but it keeps it interesting for me. I love working from home!

Learn more about Patti's businesses at the following websites:

www.pcpublications.org

www.pcpublications.net

www.historyswomen.com

www.bookbargainsandpreviews.com

www.beyondthebend.com

22

giving yourself permission to make your business a reflection of you

I have just completed the most intense period of my work-at-home life with back-to-back book deadlines and a heavy speaking schedule. I'm extremely grateful. But I've realized I can't keep up this pace and be the mom I want to be.

Ouch.

Throughout my work-at-home life I've had to curtail my ambition, say no to things I'm interested in, and force myself to be realistic about how much one woman can do from a home office. This has been difficult. But if I'm to make it to the finish line with my children and to remain sane in the process, I know it's necessary.

I also know it's necessary to give myself permission.

Permission to be myself.

Permission to be kind to myself.

Permission to let my season of mothering determine how—and how hard—I work my business.

And permission to put my business on autopilot or on hold in response to family demands or my heart's desire to be fully present and involved in my children's lives.

Perhaps you need to give yourself permission as well.

> Flexibility is essential to successfully growing a business and a family under one roof.

Nothing could have prepared me for the challenge of growing a family and a business under one roof. And despite what I've learned so far, I know there is plenty of learning still to occur. I have yet to make it through my kids' high school and college years as a work-at-home mom, and I know new trials will challenge me as a result. So I need permission.

Permission to take things as they come.

Permission to continue to combine hard work with periods of play.

Permission to allow my business to reflect who I really am rather than who I think I should be.

And permission to change my business model as my mothering seasons shift.

That's been one of my hardest lessons—realizing that flexibility is essential to successfully growing a business and a family under one roof. Though the decisions I make today will influence my business tomorrow, I need to be willing to rethink these decisions when necessary. And when what I'm currently doing no longer works, I need to be able to step back and determine what will.

And that, too, is why I need permission.

Permission to put family above work when necessary.

Permission to measure my work-at-home success by more than dollars.

Permission to set, and keep, my priorities even if they don't include the business at all.

There is a pull between the personal and the professional that challenges us as work-at-home moms. Every woman I interviewed said she struggles with maintaining the proper balance between work and family. But what if there isn't a "proper" or perfect balance? What if it's more realistic to pattern our work life after the tides—sometimes ebbing and sometimes flowing?

Anne Morrow Lindbergh challenged me in this regard with her words in *Gift from the Sea*:

> We have so little faith in the ebb and flow of life, of love, of relationships. We leap at the flow of the tide and resist in terror its ebb. We are afraid it will never return. We insist on permanency, on duration, on continuity; when the only continuity possible, in life as in love, is in growth, in fluidity—in freedom, in the sense that the dancers are free, barely touching as they pass, but partners in the same pattern. The only real security is not in owning or possessing, not in demanding or expecting, not in hoping, even. Security in a relationship lies neither in looking back to what it was in nostalgia, nor forward to what it might be in dread or anticipation, but living in the present relationship and accepting it as it is now.[1]

Perhaps it is the rising and falling of the tides—the very thing that gives us the flexibility we desire—that also simultaneously challenges us. We desire continuity yet chafe at its chains. We believe we want the freedom of fluidity, but when it comes we panic because there's nothing predictable about it.

Maybe that's what makes work at home so difficult: it's unpredictable. While clients and customers wait, we wrestle with priorities, carefully ordering them and trying to live accordingly. But there's nothing tidy about working from home. In fact, some days it's downright chaotic. How silly of me, a girl who is master of the to-do list, to think there would be anything easy about herding my brood while simultaneously responding to client and customer needs and requests. What was I thinking?

I have to believe my thinking was long term. That I took both my children's and my needs into consideration—their need for a mom who was present and my need to be the one near.

I don't think there is anything sane about working from home except maybe the fact I control my schedule and can work in my pajamas. It's the hardest thing I've ever done. But it's also the most rewarding. Somehow I've managed to swim upstream, patch together a life I love, and conquer the uncertainty that arrived when I decided to do things my way. I've stayed the course despite doubt and fear, and I've learned a lot about myself in the process. I'm still learning. These are lessons I hope to pass on to my children someday. The irony is that if I had never made the choice to become a work-at-home mom, these lessons would have been lost to me. I wonder who I would have become if I hadn't gone into business for myself?

I have no idea how long I'll work from home. I only know that the ability to do so has exceeded my wildest expectations. As I work daily to successfully grow both a business and a family under one roof, I know only one thing for sure: *I am blessed.*

How incredible it is to be present for my children while simultaneously being challenged as a professional. Until this very second I didn't realize that while growing a business I've been growing myself as well. The thought energizes me. When I left the traditional workforce, I feared I'd atrophy and stagnate. But the opposite has happened. I am not who I was, and not only because of my work.

Marissa and Mason have stretched, tested, and blessed me in ways I didn't know were possible. They are blank canvases on which I am painting, all the while knowing that though I use the same colors and brushes on each of them, the resulting pictures will be entirely unique. As I see their portraits unfold, I'm challenged to turn the brushes back on myself to see what I can add to my own life as well.

This is the gift of working at home. While molding my children, I too am being shaped into something new. Because we're under the same roof, the growth is almost imperceptible. I can barely see it, but I certainly feel it. My family and I are in this together.

It's an intimate, tender experience. It's not easy, but the rewards are worth it.

I am a wife. A mother. A CEO. I am making work at home work.

And you? It can be done, my friend. Reach for what you want, trust your instincts, follow your heart, and above all, don't be afraid to be yourself. It's what your kids need and the very thing that will make your business truly unique and successfully yours.

Lesson Learned: In addition to helping provide for your family, your business will grow you as a person.

Appendix

quick and easy dinner recipes for work-at-home moms

Recipes from *The Great American Supper Swap* by Trish Berg

Breakfast Casserole (Kelly Manley)

Ingredients:

8 eggs (slightly beaten)
6 slices white bread (cubed)
1 pound cooked sausage (drained)
2 cups milk
1 cup sharp cheddar cheese (shredded)
1 teaspoon salt
1 teaspoon dry mustard
dash of pepper

Directions:

1. Put cubed bread in a greased 9 x 13 pan.
2. Toss in cooked sausage and mix.
3. In separate bowl mix milk, salt, mustard, and eggs until blended. Pour egg mixture over sausage and bread and toss lightly.

4. Sprinkle cheese on top.

5. Cover pan with foil and refrigerate for 12 hours or overnight.

6. Bake uncovered for 35 minutes at 350 degrees. Serves 6.

Creamy Lasagna (Sylvia Koch)

Ingredients:

  1 pound lasagna noodles

  2 pounds lean ground beef

  16 ounces mozzarella cheese

  1 jar spaghetti sauce

  8 ounces cream cheese

  garlic, pepper, salt, dried green peppers, and onion powder seasoning to taste

Directions:

1. Brown ground beef and drain; add seasonings to hamburger and let simmer.

2. Place brick of cream cheese into the hamburger and let simmer until cream cheese is fully melted.

3. Cook noodles according to package directions; drain.

4. Layer in greased 9 x 13 pan: noodles, pasta sauce, and beef mixture. Repeat.

5. Bake at 350 degrees for 1 hour.

6. Serves 6.

Pan Burritos (Kelly Manley)

Ingredients:

  2 pounds ground beef

  9 large flour tortillas (9-inch)

  16 ounces shredded taco cheese

  16 ounces refried beans (warmed)

  10 ounces enchilada sauce

  3 cups water

  12 ounces tomato paste

1 garlic clove (minced)

¼ teaspoon pepper

salt to taste

taco sauce (optional)

sour cream (optional)

Directions:

1. In a saucepan, combine enchilada sauce, water, tomato paste, garlic, pepper and salt; simmer for 15 to 20 minutes.
2. In a skillet, brown and drain the beef.
3. Stir one-third of the sauce in with the beef. Spread another third on the bottom of a greased 9 x 13 baking pan.
4. Place three tortillas over sauce in pan, tearing to fit bottom of pan.
5. Spoon half of meat mixture over tortillas; sprinkle with 1½ cups cheese.
6. Add three more tortillas.
7. Spread refried beans over tortillas.
8. Top with remaining meat.
9. Sprinkle with 1½ cups cheese.
10. Layer remaining tortillas on top.
11. Top with the remaining sauce. Sprinkle with remaining cheese.
12. Bake uncovered at 350 degrees for 35 to 45 minutes. Let stand 10 minutes before cutting.
13. Serve with taco sauce and sour cream on the side if desired. Serves 6.

Parmesan Chicken Sandwiches (Audrey Doty)

Ingredients:

6 breaded chicken patties

6 slices mozzarella cheese

1 jar spaghetti sauce

6 large hamburger buns

Directions:

1. Place a single layer of chicken patties on the bottom of a greased 9 x 13 pan.
2. Pour jar of sauce over top of chicken.
3. Place a single slice of cheese on top of each patty.
4. Bake at 350 degrees for 45 minutes or until cheese melts and chicken is warm.
5. Serve on buns as sandwiches, or on the side of spaghetti. Serves 6.

Saucy Meatballs (Kathy Thut)

Ingredients:

Meatballs:

2 pounds ground beef

2 eggs

2 teaspoons salt

¼ teaspoon pepper

1 cup bread crumbs

Sauce:

14 ounces ketchup

10 ounces grape jelly

½ cup minced onion

Directions:

1. Mix meatball ingredients together and form into balls about 1 inch in diameter; place meatballs into greased 9 x 13 baking dish; set aside.
2. In large saucepan, mix ketchup, grape jelly, and onion. Cook over medium heat, stirring, until jelly is melted.
3. Pour over meatballs.
4. Can bake uncovered at 350 degrees for 45 to 60 minutes or in slow cooker on low for 4 hours. Serves 6.

Double Quick Dinner Rolls (Trish Berg)

Ingredients:

- 1 cup warm water
- 1 package active dry yeast
- 2 tablespoons sugar
- 2¼ cups flour
- 1 teaspoon salt
- 1 egg
- 2 tablespoons butter

Directions:

1. Dissolve yeast in water.
2. Add sugar, salt, egg, butter, and half of flour; blend.
3. Add remaining flour and mix.
4. Allow dough to rise for one hour. (Dough will be moist and sticky like wallpaper paste.)
5. Spoon dough into greased muffin tin.
6. Let rise again for 30 to 60 minutes.
7. Bake at 400 degrees for 15 to 20 minutes or until brown on top.
8. Brush with butter; serve warm. Makes 12 rolls.

Autumn Soup (Teri Weaver)

Ingredients:

- 1 package bacon strips
- 1 cup chopped onion
- 10 medium red potatoes
- 12 baby carrots
- 2½ cups water
- 2 tablespoons chicken bouillon
- 5 cups milk
- 2 cups frozen corn
- 1½ teaspoons pepper
- ¼ cup flour
- 12 ounces shredded cheddar cheese

Directions:

1. Cook bacon in skillet. Drain, cool, and crumble; set aside.
2. Dice potatoes and carrots; set aside.
3. In large saucepan, melt 1 teaspoon butter. Add onions, potatoes, and carrots, and sauté until tender.
4. Add water and bouillon. Bring to a boil. Reduce heat and simmer 15 to 20 minutes.
5. Stir in milk, corn, and pepper, and cook 5 minutes.
6. Combine the flour and enough water to make a paste; whisk until smooth, then add to soup.
7. Remove from heat and stir in cheese until melted.
8. At mealtime, sprinkle each bowl of soup with bacon crumbs. Serves 6.

Grape Delight (Teri Weaver)

Ingredients:

Crust:

⅓ cup butter

1 cup powdered sugar

1 package graham crackers (coarsely crushed)

Topping:

8 ounces cream cheese

1 cup powdered sugar

1 cup sour cream

8 ounces Cool Whip

Filling:

1 can frozen 100 percent grape juice

3 cans water

3 cups sugar

1 cup Clear Jel

1½ to 2 cups water

Directions:

1. Crust—In large mixing bowl, mix crushed graham crackers, ⅓ cup melted butter, and 1 cup powdered sugar. Press in greased 9 x 13 pan and set aside.
2. Cream Cheese Layer—In large mixing bowl, blend together cream cheese, 1 cup powdered sugar, sour cream, and Cool Whip. Pour over crust.
3. Grape filling—In large saucepan, combine 1 can frozen grape juice, 3 cans water, 3 cups sugar, and bring to a boil.
4. Reduce heat and slowly add 1 cup Clear Jel and 1½ to 2 cups of water while continually stirring. Mixture will thicken.
5. Bring to a boil again, then reduce heat and simmer for a few minutes.
6. Remove from heat and let cool. Pour on cream topping and refrigerate. Serves 6.

Recipes from *Once-a-Month Cooking* by Mimi Wilson and Mary Beth Lagerborg

Spaghetti Sauce

1 pound bulk Italian sausage

1½ cups finely chopped onion

1 12-ounce can tomato paste

3 28-ounce cans Italian-style or plain crushed tomatoes in puree

2 cups water

4 teaspoons minced garlic

4 bay leaves

2 tablespoons sugar

4 teaspoons dried basil leaves

2 teaspoons dried oregano leaves

4 tablespoons chopped fresh parsley

2 teaspoons salt

In a large pot, cook and stir the bulk Italian sausage with onion until the meat is brown, about 15 minutes. Drain the fat. Add remaining ingredients. Bring sauce to a boil; reduce heat. Partly cover and simmer for 1 hour, stirring occasionally.

For spaghetti, cook a 16-ounce package spaghetti noodles according to package directions and drain. Pour sauce over the noodles. Makes 8 servings (see note below).

Note: This Spaghetti Sauce recipe is one of the staple recipes of the *Once-a-Month Cooking* method. Notice that it makes 8 servings as spaghetti; however, this recipe also makes enough quantity to serve as two other meals. If you are cooking ahead, you can freeze Spaghetti Sauce for spaghetti in a 6-cup container, freeze enough in a 3-cup container for French Bread Pizza (spread it over French bread, top with desired toppings, and broil), and also freeze enough in a 2-cup container for Baked Fish in Spaghetti Sauce (pour over tilapia and bake).

Karen's Barbecued Chicken

3½ pounds boneless chicken pieces (breasts and/or thighs)
¾ cup vegetable oil
⅓ cup soy sauce
3 tablespoons Worcestershire sauce
¼ cup red wine vinegar
juice of 1 lemon
1 tablespoon dry mustard
1 teaspoon salt
2 tablespoons minced fresh parsley
½ teaspoon crushed garlic

In a one-gallon freezer bag combine all ingredients (spices together first, then add oil, then chicken). Freeze.

When thawed, remove chicken, reserving marinade. Grill over medium hot coals 15 to 20 minutes, basting frequently with reserved marinade.

Makes 5 servings.

Note: Freezing meats in marinade is great; the meat marinates as it thaws. Do not use reserved marinade from a product that has been frozen unless it is then boiled or used in the cooking process, as described here.

Mrs. Ringle's Brisket

> 1 3- to 4-pound brisket (or largest you can find)
> 2 tablespoons prepared mustard
> 1 package onion soup mix
> 4 to 5 new potatoes (optional; may be prepared separately if desired)
> flour (optional)

Place brisket fat side up in a Crock-Pot. Do not add any water or liquid. Spread brisket with mustard and sprinkle on dry onion soup mix. Cook on low 10 hours or overnight.

Skim mustard and onion seasoning from brisket and mix it with juice in the Crock-Pot. Remove brisket from Crock-Pot and allow to cool. Peel off fat and discard it; slice or shred meat. Save juices and seasonings (thicken with flour to make gravy, if desired). Divide meat and gravy in half and store in separate 1-gallon bags in freezer, one for Mrs. Ringle's Brisket and one for Hot Brisket Sandwiches.

To prepare for serving Mrs. Ringle's Brisket, thaw brisket and gravy and heat. At the same time, prepare new potatoes. Heat 1 cup salted water to a boil; add potatoes. Cover and heat until boiling; reduce heat. Simmer tightly covered until tender, 20 to 25 minutes; drain. Serve potatoes with brisket and gravy. On a different night serve Hot Brisket Sandwiches, heated and served on buns.

Makes 4 servings of Mrs. Ringle's Brisket and 4 servings of Hot Brisket Sandwiches.

Chicken Packets

    2 cups cooked, chopped chicken
    1 3-ounce package cream cheese, softened
    1 tablespoon chopped chives
    2 tablespoons milk (whole, 2 percent, or skim)
    salt to taste
    ½ cup crushed, seasoned crouton crumbs
    2 packages refrigerated crescent rolls
    ¼ cup melted butter

Mix chicken, cream cheese, chives, milk, and salt in a medium bowl (mixing with hands works best) to make filling and store in a 1-quart freezer bag. Put crouton crumbs in another 1-quart bag, attach it to bag of chicken filling, and freeze them. Refrigerate crescent rolls.

To prepare for serving, thaw chicken mixture. Unroll crescent rolls. Each tube will contain 4 rectangles of dough with a diagonal perforation. Press dough along each perforation so that the rectangle halves will not separate. Place about ¼ cup of chicken mixture into the center of each rectangle. Fold dough over the filling, and pinch the edges to seal tightly. Dip each packet in melted butter and coat with crouton crumbs. Place packets on a baking sheet. Bake in a preheated oven at 350 degrees for 20 minutes or until golden brown. Packets are good either hot or cold. Makes 8 packets, 4 to 6 servings.

Note: Chicken Packets are a perennial *Once-a-Month Cooking* kid favorite. They're great for a night when the kids and a babysitter will be preparing dinner and you will be eating out or out of town.

Aztec Quiche

    1 9-inch deep-dish frozen pie shell
    1¼ cups grated Monterey Jack cheese

¾ cup grated mild cheddar cheese

1 4-ounce can mild diced green chilies

1 cup half-and-half

3 eggs, beaten lightly

½ teaspoon salt

⅛ teaspoon ground cumin

Spread Monterey Jack cheese and half of cheddar over bottom of pie shell. Sprinkle diced chilies over cheeses. In a bowl mix the half-and-half, eggs, and seasonings. Pour carefully into pie shell. Sprinkle with remaining cheddar. Cover pie with heavy foil and freeze.

To prepare for serving, thaw pie and remove foil. Bake uncovered in a preheated oven at 325 degrees for 40 to 50 minutes.

Serve with mango and avocado slices sprinkled with lime juice. Makes 6 to 8 servings.

Note: Keep an Aztec Quiche in the freezer for a weekend breakfast or for brunch at a meeting or with friends.

Ravioli Soup

1 pound lean ground beef

¼ cup grated Parmesan cheese

¾ teaspoon onion salt

2 teaspoons minced garlic

1 tablespoon olive oil or vegetable oil

1½ cups finely chopped onion

1 28-ounce can Italian-style or plain crushed tomatoes in puree

1 6-ounce can tomato paste

1 14½-ounce can beef broth or bouillon

1 cup water

½ teaspoon sugar

½ teaspoon dried basil leaves

¼ teaspoon dried thyme leaves
¼ teaspoon dried oregano leaves
¼ cup chopped fresh parsley
1 12-ounce package plain ravioli without sauce (located in the frozen or refrigerated section)
salt
grated Parmesan cheese

Cook the ground beef in a large pot until browned, about 15 minutes. Drain the fat. Combine remaining ingredients except frozen ravioli and additional Parmesan cheese. Bring soup to a boil; reduce heat. Cover and simmer 10 minutes, stirring occasionally. Cool, put in container, and freeze.

To prepare for serving, thaw soup base and put in a large pot. Bring to a boil; reduce heat. Simmer uncovered for at least 30 minutes, stirring occasionally. Thaw and cook ravioli according to package directions until just tender. Drain ravioli; add to soup. Salt to taste. Serve with Parmesan cheese. Makes 6 servings.

French Stew

3 pounds beef stew meat
1 10¾-ounce can beef consommé
3 large peeled and sliced carrots
1 16-ounce can whole green beans, drained
8 ounces frozen small onions, separated
1 16-ounce can small peas, drained
1 16-ounce can peeled tomatoes
1 cup white wine
¼ cup minute tapioca
1 tablespoon brown sugar
½ cup fine dry bread crumbs
1 bay leaf
1 tablespoon salt, or to taste
¼ teaspoon pepper

Mix all the ingredients and cook in Crock-Pot 8 to 10 hours on low. Makes 8 servings.

Note: This stew is rich and nutritious and worthy of a company meal with fresh bread and a salad. Perfect on a chilly, dark winter's night. It freezes well.

George Romney Meatballs

Note from Mary Beth Lagerborg: This was a recipe of my mother's from the year that Mitt Romney's father was (briefly) a Republican presidential candidate.

> 1½ pounds ground beef
> 1 teaspoon salt
> dash pepper
> 1 egg
> ½ cup bread crumbs
> 2 tablespoons butter
> 2 tablespoons olive oil
> 1 cup chopped onion
> 1 cup mushroom stems and pieces
> 1 10½-ounce can beef consommé
> 1½ tablespoons flour
> 1 teaspoon salt
> ½ teaspoon caraway seed
> dash nutmeg
> 2 cups sour cream
> wide egg noodles

Shape first five ingredients into 20 small balls. In a large skillet (with a lid) sauté the chopped onion and mushrooms in the butter and olive oil until onion is transparent.

Add meatballs to the onion mixture and brown them well, turning frequently. Stir in beef consommé and simmer 30 minutes, covered.

In a small bowl combine the flour, salt, caraway seed, nutmeg, and sour cream. Add to meatballs and simmer until thickened. Serve with noodles. Makes 4 to 6 servings.

Carrie's Favorite Chicken Lasagna

> 4–5 cups cooked, diced chicken (4–5 breast halves)
> 3 cups chicken broth (use broth from cooking chicken and supplement with canned)
> 1 box lasagna noodles (Carrie leaves them uncooked, but I cook them al dente)
> ½ cup butter
> ½ cup flour
> 1 teaspoon dried basil
> 1 teaspoon salt
> ½ teaspoon pepper
> ½ cup chopped onion
> 1 24-ounce carton cottage cheese
> 1 egg
> 2 cups (8 ounces) shredded mozzarella cheese
> ¾ cup grated Parmesan cheese

Cook chicken, reserving broth. Cool and dice chicken. Meanwhile, cook lasagna until al dente. Melt butter in large saucepan over medium heat. Stir in flour, basil, salt, and pepper. Cook 1 to 2 minutes, stirring constantly. Add chicken broth and stir until smooth. Bring to boil, reduce heat, and simmer 5–8 minutes or until thick and bubbly. Stir in chicken and chopped onion. Remove from heat.

Combine cottage cheese and egg. Stir well. Layer mixture into a lightly greased 9 x 13 casserole dish as follows:

> ⅓ chicken mixture
> ½ noodles
> ½ cottage cheese mixture
> ½ mozzarella cheese

Repeat layers, ending with last ⅓ chicken mixture. Sprinkle Parmesan cheese on top. Bake at 350 degrees for 1 hour. Serves 8.

Note: This is a great entrée for company. Mary Beth suggests adding a green salad and bread.

Refrigerator Bran Muffins

Mary Beth suggests keeping batter for Refrigerator Bran Muffins in your refrigerator so you or your family members can bake healthy muffins while the coffee's brewing.

> 1 cup boiling water
> 1 cup oat bran
> 1¾ cups sugar
> ½ cup vegetable shortening (Crisco)
> 2 eggs
> 2½ cups flour
> 2½ teaspoons baking soda
> ½ teaspoon salt
> 1¾ cups buttermilk
> 2 cups All-Bran cereal (the original, "pellet" kind, not flakes)
> ¾ cup golden raisins

Pour boiling water over the oat bran and let it stand until cool. Cream together sugar and shortening. Add eggs one at a time. Add dry ingredients alternately with buttermilk. Beat until smooth.

Stir in cooled oat bran, All-Bran cereal, and raisins. Refrigerate overnight. Do not stir batter after it's refrigerated.

As needed, dip spoon into batter and fill muffin tins half full. Bake 20 minutes at 400 degrees. Batter keeps 4 to 5 weeks in refrigerator. Makes 3 dozen muffins.

Notes

Chapter 4: "I Can't Work in These Conditions!"

1. Steve Harrison's Million Dollar Author Club audio CD, Bradley Communications Corp., 2008.

Chapter 5: Guilt

1. June Walker, "Minute No. 13," June Walker Online, http://junewalkeronline.com/Index.asp?PG=69, accessed April 19, 2008.

2. Arlene Rossen Cardozo, Ph.D., *Sequencing: A New Solution for Women Who Want Marriage, Career and Family* (New York: Simon & Schuster, 1996), 245.

Chapter 8: Client Crisis—or Is It?

1. Mary Byers, *How to Say No . . . and Live to Tell About It* (Eugene, OR: Harvest House, 2006), 207.

Chapter 10: Refreshment

1. David Goetz, *Death by Suburb* (San Francisco: HarperSanFrancisco, 2006), 169.

Chapter 12: Relying on Faith to Get You Through

1. Dan Allender, Ph.D., *To Be Told: God Invites You to Coauthor Your Future* (Colorado Springs: Waterbrook Press, 2005), 125.

2. Goetz, *Death by Suburb*, 179.

Chapter 13: Accepting the At-Home CEO Mantle

1. Joseph Pine II and James H. Gilmore, *The Experience Economy* (Boston: Harvard Business School Press, 1999), 115.

Notes

Chapter 14: Professional (and Other) Advice

1. James Champey and Nitin Nohria, *The Arc of Ambition* (Cambridge, MA: Perseus Books, 2000), 182.

Chapter 15: The Tax Man Comes

1. June Walker, personal communication via email, April 7, 2008. See June's website http://junewalkeronline.com/index.asp?sPG+20.

Chapter 19: One-Page Planning

1. Leslie Charles, "2008: The Year of the Fresh Start," Why Is Everyone So Cranky? http://www.whyiseveryonesocranky.com/season/seasonal.htm, accessed March 19, 2008.

Chapter 21: Retirement Planning

1. "The Magic of Compounding," Bankrate.com, October 1, 2007, http://www.bankrate.com/brm/green/retirement/compounding_interest.asp?caret=1e.
2. As reported in Cynthia Sumner, *Dollars and Sense* (Grand Rapids: Revell, 2005), 104.
3. Ibid.
4. "Self-Employed Retirement Plan Maximum Contribution Calculator," Yahoo! Finance, 2008, http://quote.yahoo.com/calculator/career-work/qua-12.

Chapter 22: Giving Yourself Permission to Make Your Business a Reflection of You

1. Anne Morrow Lindbergh, *A Gift from the Sea* (New York: Pantheon Books, 1975), 102–3.

Mary M. Byers successfully juggles both a freelance corporate writing and speaking business and her responsibilities as a wife and mother of two school-aged children. She is the author of *The Mother Load: How to Meet Your Own Needs While Caring for Your Family* and *How to Say No . . . And Live to Tell about It*. She is also a columnist for two professional trade journals and edits two others. Byers lives in Chatham, Illinois.

Better together...

MOPS is here to come alongside you
during this season of early mothering to
give you the support and resources you
need to be a great mom.

Get connected today!